DEDICATION

For my shareholders, Naia, Finn, and Evvi

J.T.-P.

For my collaborators, Ben, Lily, and Ava

L.K.

For my sons, Lee and John

P.S.G.

CONTENTS

ACKNOWLEDGMENTS

Many thanks to ABA Book Publishing—and especially to Tim Brandhorst, Associate Director of ABA Book Publishing. Though we've never met IRL (in real life), Tim has believed enough in my ideas, even from the first e-mail exchange, to throw his support behind them, giving me the creative freedom—and time without pressure—to bring them to fruition.

Without Paul Gillies and Linsey Krolik or their enthusiasm for collaborating (Paul responded to the idea with his classic never-turn-down-an-opportunity-to-help reply, "Why not?" and Linsey said, "Sure! I've always wanted to write a book!"), this book wouldn't now be in your hands. Not only are Paul and Linsey good at what they do, they are good people. I can't imagine having gone through my life without having the opportunity to work with them or know them.

Finally, thanks to my grandmother, Thelma Tower, for showing interest in my writing projects, and to Hugh Tower-Pierce, the one who reassures me that I can get things done.

J.T.-P.

Thanks so much to Julie Tower-Pierce for inviting me to join this project. When Julie first called me about this book idea, I was immediately excited and incredibly honored. I had recently read her book *Staying at Home, Staying in the Law: A Guide to Remaining Active in the Legal Profession While Pursuing Your Dreams* and was living through the types of challenges of mothering and lawyering that Julie so eloquently writes about in that first book of hers. As we have gone through the writing process for this book, I have been so grateful to Julie for her support and guidance. Thanks also to Paul Gillies, our other wonderful coauthor. Paul's writing truly inspires me, and it amazes me how quickly he is able to get to the crux of issues. Paul has simply been a pleasure to work with.

I would also like to thank ABA Book Publishing. I can't tell you what a luxury it was to go into a first book-writing experience not only with a team of great coauthors but also with the support of this great publishing team.

I would finally like to thank my husband, Jeff Krolik, and my dad, Steve White—the two guys in my life who have been instrumental in encouraging me and challenging me over the years.

L.K.

Julie Tower-Pierce is the power behind this book. Her exuberance is compelling, addictive, and irresistible. Julie proposed the work and made initial assignments. Linsey Krolik made it glow, I put in my two cents, and Julie polished it all to the fine sheen. The book exceeds my expectations. I hope it is useful to the practice. That is its only aspiration.

We had no meetings, in the traditional sense, in this exercise in cyber writing. We did our work from our desks in three separate places, sharing ideas electronically. That was a new experience for me, and I was skeptical at first that it could work. But it did. I commend it to others.

That is the promise of the new age—that good things can come from the melding of minds unrestrained by distance and time.

Thank you ABA Publishing, Julie, Linsey, and particularly Eileen, for keeping me grounded.

P.S.G.

ABOUT THIS BOOK

Virtual Incorporation is just one example of the digital age collaboration that Vermont's legislators may have envisioned when they explored the concept of amending the state's law to allow for Digital LLC/virtual incorporation. From start to finish, this book is wholly virtually grown and reflects a geographically dispersed collaboration of human capital and energy. With Paul in Vermont, Linsey in California, and Julie in Washington, D.C., the project came to fruition through e-mail exchanges with each other and with the publisher, conference calls, "Tweets," and virtual collaboration software (Adobe Buzzword gets high marks from us). Together, without ever having met in person during this process (in fact, neither Paul nor Julie has met Linsey off-line!) we have created a collective work product for the digital age that provides the information you need to bring innovation to traditional corporate formation.

For more information about the book, visit http://www.virtualincorporationlaw.com.

FOREWORD BY BENJAMIN DURANSKE

Typically, legislation trails far behind technological progress, leaving a "wild west" mentality in the aftermath of most major technological shifts. For example, as business shifted to the Internet, this phenomenon led to domain squatting, new forms of fraud, money laundering, security failures, and privacy violations. A decade later, the law is still struggling to catch up to some of these trends. A similar shift is taking place now, as businesses embrace the evolution of the Web from a place where information is presented to a place for collaboration and creation, but somewhat remarkably, the law is ahead of the curve this time. The concept of a virtual corporation recognizes that businesses leveraging advanced collaborative tools will have special requirements, and it begins to address these needs. As such, the virtual corporation is poised to become an important and increasingly common structure as technology allows businesses to become both more collaborative and more geographically dispersed.

Before we consider the factors that are driving the creation of the virtual corporation, we should take a step back. Do you remember the Internet in 1994? You probably do not. That is because almost no one used it with any regularity. The Internet was a playground for college kids and geeks, and was hardly a forum for serious business. What is happening today is a microcosm of that shift. Bandwidth and processing power have increased sufficiently so that users can use real-time video, audio and 3D-generated content at little or no cost; advances in the standard toolbox used by web designers mean that interaction and collaboration are possible on nearly every site; and increasing availability of always-available browsers on handheld devices and ultraportable computers means that real-time collaboration is becoming the norm.

Internet trends bubble through our collective consciousness so quickly that it is almost impossible to present a timely list of them in the introduction to a printed book. However, as this foreword is being written, microblogging services like Twitter, wikis, mashups, social networking sites like Facebook, open source projects, and virtual worlds like Second Life are dominating the Internet landscape. Though the companies involved and terminology associated with them are likely to change over time, the core of each of these concepts is the same: near-instantaneous, geographically dispersed, low- or no-cost collaboration. Traditional incorporation, however, contemplates a geographically centralized location, paper-based filings, live in-person meetings, and a heavy initial focus on the distribution of shares—almost exactly the opposite of what a virtual business needs.

By contrast, virtual corporations can avoid the overhead of brick and mortar installations, leverage a talented global workforce, work with the engaged open source community, handle meetings via VOIP, video conference, or 3D generated spaces, and allow ownership to accumulate through contribution percentage, or some other measurable, not-traditional metric.

Rarely has the law been so nimble as to anticipate a need before it becomes a critical problem, but in the case of virtual corporations, that is exactly what has happened. Virtual corporations will undoubtedly become more common in the future. This book sets forth the reasons for and advantages of this important trend, and explains how companies can take advantage of important features of this new option today. It will, ultimately, help define this emerging, important field.

Benjamin Duranske is the author of Virtual Law: Navigating the Legal Landscape of Virtual Worlds, *American Bar Association, 2008.*

PREFACE

For 12 years, I was Deputy Secretary of State for Vermont, a job that gave me daily operational responsibility for the Division of Corporations. Before Vermont authorized electronic signatures, this duty included physically signing my name to dozens of articles, amendments, and dissolutions every day. What legal questions arose were addressed easily. The corporation act answered most of them. Papers flowed in and out of the office every day. There was a rhythm to it. It was a world of sagging filing cabinets, ringing telephones, and hardworking clerks. The hardest question was whether one company name was too much like another to be approved.

In the vault of the State Archives, there were musty volumes of early corporation records, often done by hand or on early typewriters. These records of mostly defunct corporations served as a reminder that the state's role in incorporating businesses had remained unchanged for a long time. But change did come. First there was microfilm, on which reels of paper records were stored, and made accessible, but only for the division's use. Later, computers were brought in, first only to produce certificates and store basic information; then allowing access to that information over the Net.

Vermonters have been organizing as corporations since 1780, and the state's control over those corporations was at first rather limited. For years the only way a corporation could be established was by charter, as a special act of the legislature, and printed in the legislative record for all to see. Vermont's first general corporation law was enacted in 1853.[1] After that, incorporators could bypass the legislature if they chose. The law did not mandate administrative organization of corporations, however, and still the legislature

[1] Vermont Laws of 1853, No. 71. The first general corporation law was enacted in Connecticut, in 1837, followed by Maryland (1838), New Jersey (1846), Pennsylvania (1849), Indiana and Massachusetts (1851), and Virginia (1852). Adolph Berle, Jr., & Gardner C. Means, The Modern Corporation and Private Property 136 (Columbia University Council for Research in The Social Sciences 1933).

was hounded by those seeking special favors through charters and amendments. Vermont tried to change the law—largely as a way of limiting the number and aggressiveness of lobbyists—but not until 1913, when a constitutional amendment was enacted, was the transition to the executive branch and to administrative oversight of private for-profit corporations complete. Since that time, corporations have been governed by general statute. When changes are needed in corporation law, they are applied universally, by amending the code.

Innovation ensued. With the development and enactment of alternatives to the traditional corporation, the alternatives were designed to reduce the formalities and increase the flexibility of the historic model business organization, which included the close corporation and the limited liability corporation—and in the nonprofit world, the L3C, designed to offer modest charitable undertakings an opportunity to organize under the LLC model. Every few years, something new has come along in response to the needs of the marketplace. States like Vermont are always asking, "What is it you want from the business community?" In the rather stale world of business organization, imagination abounds.

Although national models of corporation laws have been enacted from time to time, not until 2008 has Vermont enjoyed the status of a leader in corporation law reform—a prize usually claimed by Delaware, Nevada, or other progressive incorporation states. Into this small corner of the world has come an opportunity to meld the worlds of corporation law and the electronic age in what has been called the "Virtual Corporation."

INTRODUCTION

The Corporation

Chief Justice John Marshall described corporations as artificial beings, mere creatures of the law, possessing only powers conferred by charter or general corporation law.[1] Corporations built offices, ran factories, engaged in high finance; but what constituted the corporation has until now consisted largely of a set of papers neatly filed in a special folder within the state office responsible for keeping records, and a larger set of records, including those not filed publicly, in the principal office. These records memorialize the doings of the corporation, preserving the decisions and ensuring their enforceability. In other words, corporations have traditionally been paper institutions, created on paper, kept in good standing by paper (official or corporate), and remembered on paper in the form of minutes, resolutions, certifications, and governance documents. Lawyers who have built careers in corporation law have bookshelves lined with corporation "kits"—the names of the entities printed nicely on the spine—containing the minutes, blank stock certificates, articles, an official seal, and bylaws. The lawyer's job has often consisted largely of reminding the individuals involved to act like a corporation, and of drafting the ephemera that accompany the active life of the business. Attending annual meetings, advising shareholders and boards on what can and cannot be done, involved simply reading the bylaws, in the context of the general corporation law in place at the time.

Corporation law is about governance. Articles of association and bylaws are the operating manuals for this choice of business organization, under the framework of a state's corporation laws and the federal tax code. State laws often allow corporations to opt in or out of particular provisions, such as the use of proxies or the

[1] The Trustees of Dartmouth College v. Woodward, 17 U.S. 518 (1819).

definition of majority and minority powers; but the code has been the central nervous system of the corporation since the middle of the 19th century. Anyone practicing corporation law with a copy of the code deskside risked worries about malpractice.

The computer has changed the experience of incorporating. Many states presently allow corporations to be formed online, with an electronic signature and a credit card or a book account. The process still takes a few days, unless you are willing to pay a special expedited service fee that is available in some jurisdictions. There are companies that will form your corporation for you, for a fee.[2] A whole industry has built up to promote the corporation form, flogging the advantages of limited liability as a statutory form of insurance.

In an age of uncertain financial stability, the protection offered by the corporation, as opposed to the partnership or sole proprietorship, is too compelling to ignore. With its cousin, the limited liability company (considered by some as "corporation lite"), the corporation offers people a method for governing investments, resources, and profits in accord with the amount of investment in the venture—whether financial or other commitment—and safely, placing only the investment at risk.

What Vermont Has Done

During the 2008 session of the General Assembly, Vermont adopted NYC Law School Professor David Johnson's plan for a virtual corporation law.[3] The idea goes far beyond the mechanics of forming a corporation. Professor Johnson's vision is the creation of a model of business organization that is in sync with the turbulent world of software development. He foresees the end of the hierarchical governance model with its investment in the structure of a directors and officers. The new law frees virtual corporations from unnecessary formality. It embraces flexibility as a principal virtue. Vermont becomes the most tolerant of corporation law states under this concept.

While the pure idea of a complete Internet corporation experience through the Vermont Secretary of State's home page must

[2] *See* http://www.attorneyscorpserv.com (last visited May 1, 2009).

[3] "An act relating to miscellaneous tax amendments," Laws of 2007 (Adj. Sess.), No. 190, Sections 74–100.

await software development and installation, Vermont corporation law changed on July 1, 2008, in substantive ways—all in the name of ensuring the greatest flexibility and adaptability in organizing and running a corporation. All corporations, not just those calling themselves virtual corporations, benefit from these amendments. The advances in corporation design, notice and meeting requirements, and document creation, storage, and retrieval are now applicable to any Vermont corporation.

The premise of these changes is a refreshingly candid look at the old ways, coupled with an almost casual willingness to jettison anything that is not necessary. Freedom can be liberating, or it can be impracticably disorderly. This model trusts incorporators to know the difference and choose the forms they believe are necessary, without any worry about tradition or formalities that make no sense. At its heart, the idea is anticorporate. It can seem almost Reichian—a flower stuck in the barrel of a corporate rifle—and because it is new, it seems vital and invigorating. The only risk to its success is a lack of care and a lack of imagination.

The virtual corporation, according to Professor Johnson, will thrive because entrepreneurs of ideas and products on the Net will find each other. They will appreciate how they can work together and then almost seamlessly incorporate in Vermont, in ways they find reflect their needs, with far fewer intrusions from state corporation law as to governance, decision making, and distribution of profits than in other states. The parties won't have to wait for weeks. They can make agreements and decisions at their own speed, in their own workspaces and time zones. It won't matter when the corporation office opens. It won't matter what the code says you must do, because you may make it up as you go along. The law will be there if needed; but the answers to the resolution of disputes will be found principally in the operating agreement, not in some starchy corporation code.

The Vermont Town Meeting

The idea of the virtual corporation is unintentionally derivative of the Vermont town meeting. Vermont is the home of direct democracy. At town meetings, voters adopt the municipal budget, set into motion their own tax rate, decide when taxes are due and the penalty and interest for late payments, establish salaries for officials, and enact local legislation such as zoning bylaws. The people control the public corporation. The select board or school board is bound by the decisions made at a town meeting.

The virtual corporation model dispenses with the board. It allows the shareholders—the stakeholders—to make the decisions that count, leaving the administration of those decisions to others. The oligarchy of a board and officers is eliminated.

No corporation is a perfect democracy. Ownership determines proportionate power, but the principle of a direct connection between what you own and what you control is maintained with the virtual corporation. Every important decision is made by those who have taken the risk of investment. It's an old, new idea.

The Virtual Corporation

The virtual corporation is not an entirely new idea. More than 15 years ago, the idea of networking and "virtualization" was the subject of discussion in England and on the continent.[4] Networking, of course, is as old as the human species.

The traditional corporation is based on the raising, expenditure, and distribution of capital, in the form of shares of stock. Virtual corporations start with the premise that the participants have already invested in capital; what they contribute to the joint venture are the products of their imagination and genius—what Professor Johnson calls the "pooling of time and effort."[5] Traditional corporations have principal offices in the state of incorporation, formal notices for annual and special meetings, and reams of pro forma paperwork. Virtual corporations may physically reside in the ether, hold meetings by audio or video conferencing or even e-mail or live chat, and avoid the need for the white tablecloth and the silverware of corporate formality.

The virtual corporation model adapts the operating agreement first authorized by law in the limited liability company model and offers incorporators opportunities to establish relationships that fit the needs and style of Internet business life. Lighter, easier,

---

[4] W.H. DAVIDOW & M.S. MALONE, THE VIRTUAL CORPORATION: STRUCTURING AND REVITALIZING THE CORPORATION FOR THE 21ST CENTURY (Harper Business 1992). *See also* http://www.skyrme.com/resource/virtres.htm#Davidow (last visited May 1, 2009).

[5] David R. Johnson, *Virtual Companies*, http://dotank.nyls.edu/june18virtualcorp.html (last visited May 1, 2009).

quicker, smoother; operating all night, in the present, without a glass-and-steel edifice to call home; in sync with its founders' lifestyles; the virtual corporation gives entrepreneurs the template for organizing joint projects safely and reliably.

Although the idea is not expressly included in the Vermont legislation, the virtual corporation may be best implemented by the creation of a "hosting company," established in Vermont for the purpose of providing a playing field where different parties can merge their interests, combine their strengths, and create products and systems under the alias of a new business entity that is capable of borrowing money without undue risk to the investors and avoiding worries about being mistaken for a partnership. To date, no hosting corporation has been formed; but work is under way to ensure the structure is there when the first entrepreneurs arrive to realize the full potential of the virtual corporation.

The purpose of this book is to introduce the new law to practitioners. Like all new ideas, when put into practice, this one is certain to evolve over time. The creative energy spawned by the freedom offered through Vermont law will surprise all of us. This is just the beginning.

Caveat lector: the language of the virtual corporation may sound vaguely subversive. This is not your father's corporation. The idea eschews the old hierarchies of the traditional corporation. It regards nothing as sacred except success. It fantasizes about communities of interest, the synergy of collaborating minds and skills, and freedom to create power and wealth without the trappings of convention. It may seem as if the underlying capitalism inherent in the corporation has given way to a new infatuation with democracy, with its power sharing and plain speaking. Never forget what century you live in or the likelihood of change. Those who succeed are those who can adapt.

CHAPTER ONE

Virtual Incorporation: Move Over, Delaware . . . A New Business Form for Digital Age Start-Ups

Delaware has long been known as the state for businesses to incorporate in, a corporate haven of sorts. According to Delaware's Division of Corporations, more than 50 percent of all publicly traded companies in the United States—including 63 percent of the Fortune 500—have chosen Delaware as their state of incorporation.[1]

---

[1] State of Delaware Division of Corporations, http://www.corp.delaware.gov/aboutagency.shtml (last visited May 1, 2009).

Delaware is seen to provide businesses with a high degree of flexibility in formation and in corporate governance matters. Add this latitude to some potentially important tax benefits for out-of-state corporations, a large body of corporate case law, and a seemingly streamlined dispute resolution, and Delaware easily becomes a place where corporations want to be.

But Delaware is not the only business-friendly, progressive state in the United States. Nevada counts itself as another corporate haven, as does California—which may explain the many start-up companies located in these states. And now, we can add Vermont to the list.

A new statutory development makes it potentially possible for Vermont to emerge as a digital age corporate haven with a business form for digital age start-ups. With the passing of H.458 in Vermont[2] on June 6, 2008—amending the limited liability company statutes found at Sec. 74. 11 V.S.A. § 3001—Vermont stands a chance at becoming the "new Delaware" for incorporation. Vermont now offers revolutionary corporate flexibility to attract even the most loosely formed Internet-based "virtual corporations." Other states may also be considering similar provisions, but Vermont is currently at the forefront of this movement for "virtual incorporation" tailored to digital age start-ups.

What Exactly Is a Virtual Incorporation?

Googling the definition of a virtual incorporation or virtual corporation will net you business marketing descriptions like these:

From Dictionary.com Webster's New Millennium Dictionary of English, Preview Edition: A virtual corporation is "a business organization that exists mainly on the Internet and does business through a Web site and email, relying on telecommunications and computer technology for its operation, including telecommuting and videoconferencing; also a group of

[2] See Appendix A for the entire text of the amendment.

independent companies that function as one entity through telecommunications and computer technology."[3]

From the PCMag.com Encyclopedia: A virtual company is "an organization that uses computer and telecommunications technologies to extend its capabilities by working routinely with employees or contractors located throughout the country or the world. Using e-mail, faxes, instant messaging, data and videoconferencing, it implies a high degree of telecommuting as well as using remote facilities."[4]

From Answers.com: A virtual corporation is a "cooperative agreement between two or more business entities to combine their resources in order to achieve a shared goal. It is called a virtual corporation because by bringing in additional partners, unlimited skills and resources can be pooled. Virtual corporations are usually temporary, and the partnership dissolves once the shared goal is reached. For example, several computer hardware and computer software manufacturers might form a virtual corporation in order to produce a product that exploits a particular market niche such as a PC system for the real estate industry. Computer, cable television, telephone, and communications industry companies have formed virtual corporations to exploit interactive television technologies known as the electronic highway."[5]

In this book, however, we are talking about virtual incorporation in the legal sense. Some guidance can be found from the Vermont Secretary of State Corporations Division, which describes its Digital Corporations/LLC Act "as allow[ing] the company and their participants to dictate almost all of the terms of their internal organizational and operational communications between them by means of a digital operating agreement—thus dispensing with the standard paper-based format. Participants are free to agree upon

[3] Dictionary.com, "virtual corporation," in Webster's New Millennium Dictionary of English, Preview Edition (v 0.9.7), http://dictionary.reference.com/browse/virtualcorporation, *available at* http://dictionary.reference.com (last visited May 1, 2009).

[4] PCMag.com, "virtual company," in the PCMag.com Encyclopedia, http://www.pcmag.com/encyclopedia_term/0,2542,t=virtual+corporation&i=53904,00.asp (last visited May 1, 2009).

[5] Answers.com, "virtual corporation," http://www.answers.com/topic/virtual-corporation (last visited May 1, 2009).

the terms of their relationship, and how the company is to be governed, the economic relationships between them, how meetings are to be conducted, and other internal matters."[6]

In effect, "virtual incorporation" affords a company the traditional legal protections of LLC status, while providing enhanced flexibility and corporate control conducive to innovative and creative relationships and methods of operating in a digital era.

See the accompanying box for our legal definition of virtual incorporation.

Virtual Incorporation Defined

The formation of a limited liability entity *without* the requirements of

- a physical location or address,
- capitalization in the form of money or property contributed to the business, or
- a hierarchical management structure

and *with* the ability to make electronic filings and engage in electronic communications for its corporate governance.

One important distinction between the definitions currently found on the Internet for virtual companies or virtual corporations and the legal definition for virtual incorporation that we provide above is the concept of this virtual company or corporation being a *limited liability entity*. We assume the practitioner reading this book is familiar with the concepts and motivations behind incorporation for business founders into limited liability entities such as C corporations, S corporations, limited liability companies (LLCs), and other limited liability entities for the purposes of limiting the actors' personal liability regarding the activities and liabilities of the business. This is a key distinction because it means that these virtual corporations are legally recognized entities. That is, the virtual entity has a legal personhood, beyond that of a contract or agreement, and such legal personhood is recognized by other corporations and in other states.

Another important distinction between the business definition of "virtual corporations" and the legal definition above for

[6] Vermont Secretary of State Corporations Division, http://www.sec.state.vt.us/corps/index.htm (last visited May 1, 2009).

"virtual incorporation" is that the virtual corporation entity is not temporary (although it may have transient contributors). In Vermont, for instance, the virtual corporation is legally an LLC. This lack of required hierarchical structure allows for the company to easily continue as a legal person, even as the actors change over time, at least until the company is legally dissolved.

When we talk about virtual corporations as legal entities, there is no requirement for these companies to conduct all their activities online or virtually—although that might often be the case in practice. The idea is one of flexibility and removing requirements of physicality.

We will go into the specifics of the definition in the following sections—especially as they may relate to the practitioner's client, who may be considering the virtual corporation as the entity for its business.

Note that this book does *not* discuss contractual methods of creating a "virtual company"[7] or partnership or collaborator agreements. Such arrangements are not limited liability entities. This book is limited to discussion of entities that provide limited liability protection to the company's actors and legal personhood for the entity.

How Did Virtual Incorporation Come About?

Virtual incorporation has come about due to the rise in collaborative endeavors that have been possible through the widespread use of the Internet in our world and in business. Software development; collaborative blogging, content creation, and publishing; and Internet businesses are all examples of collaborative endeavors.

Examples of collaborative businesses

- Software development and open source
- Internet businesses
- Collaborative blogs, publications, and wikis
- Businesses operating in virtual words (e.g., Second Life)

[7] For an example of something that promotes the creation of "virtual companies" that is contractual only, *see* FairSoftware.net at http://www.fairsoftware.net (last visited May 1, 2009).

The comprehensive Wikipedia encyclopedia is a perfect example of a virtual collaborative work that is a labor of love—with changing contributors and contribution levels, without a central physical location, with contributors located all around the world, and without the need for capital funding because most of what is contributed is time rather than money.

Likewise, some of the most successful blogs and other publications are created and operate collaboratively, to reduce the pressure on a single person and to vary the perspectives, opinions, and content. Because the creation and publication are done online, there is often no need for a physical office or investment of any large amount of money for expenditures.

Before virtual incorporation—and still in many states—collaborative groups basically had two different legal options. They could be classified as partnerships (sometimes intentionally; but often such classification is by default if the participants have not chosen an entity), in which case the participants do not enjoy limited personal liability. Or, the group could decide to incorporate as a limited liability entity (a C corp, S corp, or LLC, usually), spending time and money trying to fit themselves into a corporate box that may not truly meet their needs. There is a need for a more flexible limited liability form for collaborative projects that have more transient participants, are less capital based, and are less physical in nature.

Why the Change from Traditional Business Formation Options, and What Is Its Legal Significance?

Traditional business formation options offering limited liability protection—corporations and LLCs, mainly—require the incorporator to list a physical address of its headquarters, the authorized number of shares the company is authorized to issue in exchange for money, and its members (for an LLC) or its directors and officers (for a corporation). These things can be awkward for contributors to a project that is being developed or operated virtually. Many collaborative projects created and operated largely online have no physical address, although a participant's home address could be used. In fact, the contributors are often located in various places—around town, in different states, or even in different countries. Also, because operating expenses are often minimal, there is no need for capital in the form of exchanging cash for shares. Participants' contributions likely take the form of time, effort, and expertise contributed rather than money or property. The hierarchical structure of traditional corporations or LLCs may not fit the working model of a collaborative virtual business in which the people actively participating or contributing are self-selected in the first place—and their effort level may change quickly as the needs of the business change.

The legal significance of virtual incorporation is that participants in these collaborative projects can enjoy limited liability for the activities of the business as well as the flexibility so essential to their business. A virtual business is able to be a recognized legal entity, so that it can enter into contracts and be "officially" on the radar. Virtual incorporation gives participants credibility and security while allowing the business to function in a meaningful way. It also provides the incorporating state with revenues, in the form of taxes and filing fees, and the ability to track these types of businesses that may have been operating "outside the system."

How Are Virtual and Traditional Incorporations Different?

There are several important differences between virtual and traditional incorporations. We start with the requirements for both a traditional incorporation and a virtual incorporation.

Requirements for a Traditional Incorporation

- Name of company
- Physical address of the company's headquarters
- Name and address of an agent for service of process
- Names and addresses of directors and officers for a corporation or members for a LLC (This information is routinely updated in statement of information or other filing, which is filed with the state of incorporation.)
- Number of shares authorized to be issued for the corporation or the capital accounts for LLC
- Paper-based filings
- In-person board and shareholder meetings (Although many states allow for meetings to occur via electronic transmission, such as a teleconference, provided that

certain parameters are met and that actions or resolutions are taken by unanimous written consent of all directors or shareholders.)

Requirements for a Virtual Incorporation

(Looking at Vermont's limited liability company statutes, as amended in June 2008 for digital corporations)

- Name of company
- Name and address of an agent for service of process
- Electronic filings of formation and registration documents
- Meetings conducted in person or through the use of an electronic medium (Even asynchronous online communications are permitted for decision making and record keeping.)

As you can see, the concept of virtual incorporation is focused on removing traditional requirements of physicality, hierarchy, and capital infusion. New requirements are not imposed; *flexibility* is the paramount theme of virtual incorporation.

What Are the Key Differences between Traditional Incorporations and Virtual Corporations?

1. *Location of actors.* In a traditional incorporation, the actors are centralized and have physical office space. Although a home address of one of the actors in a traditional corporation could be selected as the physical address for the traditional corporation's principal office, such an address must still be listed with the state of incorporation. Contrast this requirement with that of a virtual incorporation, which needs only an agent for service of process—and can hire a corporate agent service to do so. A virtual corporation often has no need for a "principal office," because contributors are decentralized and geographically dispersed. The actors in a virtual corporation may engage largely (or solely) in online communication. The virtual corporation itself has a dynamic existence in that the company is physically located wherever the contributors open their laptops and have an Internet connection or make a phone call.

2. *Capital.* Traditional forms of capitalization are money or property (valued at fair market value, for instance), in exchange for shares of the corporation. In a virtual corporation, capital could take many forms—intellectual capital, expertise, time, reputation, mutual ratings of contributor's contributions, attention, or effort. Also, in a virtual corporation, the contributors may already own computers and have Internet connections. These are pooled resources that may remain the property of individual contributors.
3. *Organization/management structure.* A traditional corporation has a hierarchical management structure, either a board of directors for a corporation or managing members for an LLC. Authority is then delegated to individuals, such as officers and other employees or consultants, to act as agents of the company. In a virtual corporation, the management consists of group-based decision making. The participants self-select by volunteering to do particular tasks or taking the lead on major projects. Because effort and attention vary depending on business need, the actors in a virtual corporation are often changing or in flux throughout the company's lifetime.
4. *Filings and record keeping.* A traditional corporation's filings and records are paper based. In a virtual corporation, filings are done online, and record keeping of decisions can be in electronic form. Digital signatures are acceptable.
5. *Meetings.* In-person meetings are required in a traditional corporation, except in states that allow for actions taken with written consent without a meeting or that allow for meetings via electronic transmission (e.g., videoconference) in some situations and provided certain conditions are met. Vermont's digital corporations law provides a new definition for "meeting," which is "any structured communications conducted by participants in person or through the use of electronic or telecommunications medium permitting simultaneous or sequentially structured communications for the purpose of reaching a collective agreement."[8] This kind of communication is really

[8] VT. STAT. ANN. Sec. 74. 11, § 3001 (26).

quite wide open and different from the traditional methods, even where electronic transmission for meetings is allowable. For example, cutting-edge technology and communication tools, such as Twitter, or virtual worlds, such as Second Life, can serve as the media for transacting corporate business. Again, the flexibility for virtual corporations is apparent in this language of the statute.

The following table presents some of the other comparisons we can make about traditional and virtual incorporations.

Traditional versus Virtual Corporations		
	Traditional	**Virtual**
Location of actors	Centralized, physical office(s) in one or more location(s)	Decentralized, dispersed, dynamic (wherever contributors open their laptops)
Selection of actors	Employees/ consultants selected by founders or managers	Self-selected contributors
Finances/ Capital	Money and/ or property are needed as capital contributions	No need for cash infusion—capital is in the form of intellectual capital, expertise, time, reputation, mutual ratings of contributor's contributions, attention, and/or effort
Resource ownership	Owned by the business	Pooled, remains the property of individual contributors
Type of business	Development/ manufacture/sale of physical goods, linear nature	Internet, service, business of a collaborative nature

	Traditional	Virtual
Management structure	Hierarchical, management appointments are long term	Transient participants who are self-selected and make group decisions
Voting	Per member or per share	Varied voting structures (e.g., based on ratings)
Meetings	In person, specific time and place	Online, electronic transmission (may even be a sequence of e-mails rather than happening at a specific time)
Filings	Paper-based through snail mail (although more and more states do have some electronic filings)	Online, electronic
Stability as a limited liability entity	Tried and true	New, some unknowns; untested in the courts

Is Virtual Incorporation Right for Your Client?

Every client is different, so the practitioner's analysis will depend on asking the right questions and interpreting the client's answers correctly. The checklists on the following pages lay out the key pieces of information you will need, along with interactions and discussions with your client, to determine whether virtual incorporation is right for your client.

CHECKLIST: Should you take your client in the direction of virtual incorporation?

If your client answers YES to many of the following items, virtual incorporation may a good option for his or her business:

✓ There is a founder or founders; but the founder's efforts and contributions may vary or even drop off over time, and the efforts of other contributors will play a large role in business operations.

✓ The contributors to the product or service are geographically dispersed.

✓ The contributors to the product or service are self-selected.

✓ The business has a dynamic existence; there is no intention or need for a physical office.

✓ There is no intention or need to raise capital in the form of money (in the form of venture capital or otherwise) or have property contributed to the company.

✓ The founders/contributors will be using pooled resources (e.g., computers and Internet connections) that remain the property of the individual contributors.

✓ The founder(s) wishes to share the proceeds of the business with its contributors on the basis of effort, reputation, time, intellectual capital, or expertise contributed.

✓ The founders/contributors wish to make decisions together, with all contributors having some sort of vote, rather than to have a management team of a select few make all decisions.

✓ The business is interstate or even international in nature in that there will not be a state(s) where most of the business will be taking place.

✓ The founders/contributors are comfortable with filing paperwork online, holding meetings in electronic format, and maintaining records for the business in a secure electronic form.

✓ The founders are comfortable with being a sort of "guinea pig" with a new form of business entity.

On the flip side, if your client answers YES to many of the following items, virtual incorporation may NOT be a good option for his or her business:

- ✓ The founder(s) of the business intend to dedicate themselves to managing and operating the business for a fairly long time.
- ✓ The contributors to the product or service are geographically centralized.
- ✓ The contributors to the product or service are selected by the founder(s)/manager(s) of the business.
- ✓ The business requires a physical office (for instance, if the business sells physical products that require manufacturing and shipping from specific physical locations).
- ✓ The founder(s) need to raise capital in the form of money to operate the business.
- ✓ The founder(s) intend to or need to purchase significant resources that will be the property of the business.
- ✓ The founder(s) do not wish to share the proceeds of the business with contributors on the basis of effort or other valuation, but wish to pay contributors in the form of traditional salaries, consulting fees, stock option plans, and/or bonus structures.
- ✓ The founder(s) wants to have a traditional hierarchical structure for decision making in that a select few managers will make the decisions for the business and pass directives down to employees.
- ✓ The business will be focused in one or more state(s) where most of the business will be taking place.
- ✓ The founders are not comfortable with filing paperwork online, holding meetings in electronic format, and maintaining records for the business in a secure electronic form.
- ✓ The founder(s) do not wish to take risks on a new form of business entity.

CHAPTER TWO

The Nuts and Bolts of Virtual Incorporation

Your law office opens, and your advertising explains you offer services to corporations. Clients come to you with an idea. It's a promising idea, one that could grow into something of great value. These clients want your advice on which business organization to adopt. You open your sample case and explain the various choices of business organization. Here we can see the traditional C or S corporations, the limited liability partnership, the limited liability corporation, and—yes, something new here—the virtual corporation. But which of these forms is best suited for your client's needs? That is the first question you must answer.

Most new businesses intentionally avoid the partnership—the one without limits, at least. Partnership today is more an epithet associated with bad examples of people who chose to do business with each other without knowing what to expect from the consequences of decisions made by one *partner* without the knowledge or support of the others. In some cases, people encounter unexpected liabilities by not understanding the venture is a partnership.

The decision on which entity to choose is not purely discretionary. Accountants and tax advisors play an important role in the choice of the remaining options. The limited liability partnership is favored by professionals (along with its once trendy professional corporation). The limited liability company (LLC) has enjoyed the latest popularity and is often recommended to those who want to shield their personal property from exposure in the owning and operating of real estate ventures.

But here is the newest product—the virtual corporation. It may be just what your clients are looking for in a business model (see Chapter 1). Suppose they are convinced to try it out. What do you have them do next?

What Now?

Pre-Incorporation Planning and Decision Making

Filing articles of incorporation as a virtual corporation is the last chapter in the first volume of a new corporation's life. Before that happens, the participants need to talk to each other to decide certain critical questions (see Appendix B, Example Client Intake Information). As with all ventures, some of the first questions to address are what the players want to achieve with this new business and who should make the important decisions affecting the company.

Nobody has time to reinvent the idea of the corporation. Old formulas, templates, and models usually get the players past the formalities to the critical decisions on how much money or effort each one will contribute. The better practice is to make those decisions well before contacting any state office.

The form used by Vermont includes a space for participants to state the purpose of the corporation. The box, which allows only a few words, is used largely for statistical purposes. In Vermont, a corporation need not be any more specific than that; it essentially can choose to state no purpose beyond the powers granted by law to all corporations. But there is no prohibition against asserting a purpose—and good reason to focus on a statement of purpose—in the operating agreement, if not in the articles. In practical terms, however, all organizers must first agree how to spell success—before building any edifice, virtual or corporeal. That goal need not be disclosed publicly in any filing with the state.

Choosing a Name

Vermont law requires the names of new corporations to be "distinguishable from, and not the same as, deceptively similar to, or likely to be confused with or mistaken for any" other name previously granted or registered by the Vermont Secretary of State.[1] There is no mystery to this process. Close calls are likely rejected. Before filing any articles, incorporators can surf through the electronic files of entities registered by the Secretary and easily predict whether their choice will pass muster.[2] The files contain very basic information about the various business entities, including name, address, registered agent, and officials.

The familiar names are taken. The longer the name or the more creative, the less likely the state is to reject it. Don't confuse the corporation name with the name you may intend to use to sell a product or advance a project. A corporation can hold various business or trade names for that purpose. Reject cute names. Say it aloud ten times, and imagine reading it ten times more than that, and you may realize how sorry you'll be when your venture takes off, wearing a banner that detracts from the seriousness or the purpose of the investment. Think how others will regard you, not as individuals but by a moniker that expresses the personality of the corporation. Consider conducting a simultaneous domain name search to see whether you are able to secure the name online; while the domain name need not necessarily match your filed name, the availability of a domain name may impact your decision (e.g., avoiding brand confusion).

Board or No Board

In a traditional corporation model, filling the seats on the initial board of directors is an early chore. A board directs the corporation. It sets policy and makes the essential decisions. Placing these powers in a board carefully selected for its various members' experience and skills instills respect for the corporation and soundness in decision making. Even if you choose to forgo a formal board of directors, you may wish to enlist a group of advisers to assist you in business planning. But this new age of digital corporations may not be patient enough to await the assembling of a board—or comfortable with assignment of decision making to a board.

With the new Vermont digital corporation, the organizers may dispense with the board in favor of any other arrangement that

---

[1] VT. STAT. ANN. tit. 11A, § 4.01.

[2] Vermont Secretary of State Corporations Division, http://www.sec.state.vt.us/corps/index.htm (last visited May 1, 2009).

makes sense for making corporate decisions. It can change its mind, and its incorporeal form, by amending its articles at any time; but the law now eliminates the need for that organizational model as a prerequisite to organization. The one-person corporation, the same individual holding all offices, is possible now. The choices of organizational structure are left to the organizers and to the seminal operating agreement that is the heart of the virtual corporation concept. Vt. Stat. Ann. 11A § 7.32.

Tradition deserves respect, but form may now follow function in the organization of a virtual corporation. The only limits are the creativity of its organizers. Suppose there are three of you, each with something valuable to offer to a new venture. Shares or other indicia of ownership will be issued (the word "points" is often used to reflect the break with tradition), but how will power be allocated? In the traditional corporation, the shareholders elect the board members, and the board rules. In a nontraditional model, the shareholders may make all the decisions, as long as their numbers are not unwieldy and the governing document is clear enough to allow business to go on without the intrusions of formalities in the corporation form.

These new freedoms are not extended to foreign corporations under Vermont law. Only those organized in Vermont may enjoy the advantages of electronic filing of articles. Vt. Stat. Ann. 11A, §§ 1.20, 16.22.

Pre-Incorporation and Operating Agreements

Vermont law does not regulate pre-incorporation agreements or operating agreements. That is the point of the virtual corporation idea. You can design a new structure, or adapt or adopt any existing model, and what you adopt does not have to be filed with the Corporations Division. The operating agreement is your business.

The operating agreement is the centerpiece of the virtual corporation, so its creation must precede the filing of any articles of incorporation. There are resources on the Net already in place to assist.[3] Models appear at the end of this book (see Appendix D). Deciding what the operating agreement must contain involves

[3] Do Tank and the Democracy Design Workshop, http://dotank.nyls.edu/Visual Corporation.html (last visited May 1, 2009).

analyzing the realities of the venture. Think through a variety of scenarios, each involving a vision of success or failure, to test the resiliency of the organization of the virtual corporation. What if this happens? What do we do about it? Where in the operating agreement are the answers? Suppose the venture folds or fails—how will the remaining assets be distributed? Suppose we succeed beyond our wildest dreams? How will we evolve?

Because the virtual corporation was created to address a specific need in the marketplace for ventures created out of other, established ventures, organizers will need to understand the powers and limitations of constituent parts before forging a new identity. Organizers may need to adapt their structures to ensure the digital corporation has the freedom to succeed in fulfilling the dreams, while keeping the promises, of those involved.

What you contribute determines what you can take out. That is a principle (for many years, merely an ideal) as old as civilization itself.[4] How to assign the value of contributions is the key question. When money is the medium of exchange, the share is set at a fixed or fluctuating market value and may be conveyed, exchanged, or sold. The virtual corporation model intuits a different model. The value of what shareholders contribute need not be based on a financial contribution, but on the collective (majoritarian) appraisal of what a member brings to the association.

Anti-takeover provisions in operating agreements are authorized by Vermont law and ought to be considered to protect the venture's integrity. Shares may be sold; but the agreement may grant the corporation or its shareholders rights of first refusal and may commit the shareholder to a specific method of valuation for the shares.

Articles

The filing of articles of association during the last century and before that time was based on the charter model, where incorporators listed details on the operation of the corporation. This model has been replaced in recent years by forms, filed with the Secretary of State's office, consisting of basic information—the name of the

[4] Abraham Lincoln defined slavery in his debate with Douglas in these words: "You work and toil and earn bread, and I'll eat it."

corporation, the names of the initial board of directors, the name of the registered agent, and the address of the principal office. As noted earlier, purpose need not be stated in the articles.

Articles must prescribe the number of shares, if there are to be shares. They must also differentiate the classes of shares, explaining the rights and responsibilities of different classes, including voting rights and details on the distribution of net assets upon dissolution, unless the articles assign those rights to the board of directors.[5] Number of shares is a self-imposed limitation on dividing the ownership and control of the corporation among various shareholders. The number cannot be increased without amending the articles, by a process that also requires approval by the Secretary.

Articles are submitted to the Secretary of State using a dedicated form, which may be accessed on the Net.[6] The articles are filed before the issuance of any stock.

With the virtual corporation, the articles will not list shares. That apportionment of ownership, as measured by control and an enforceable right to share in profits, is done through the operating agreement.

Bylaws

Bylaws are the operating manual of the corporation. Usually they start with a template, adapted over the years to the various needs of the parties, listing the central principles for the organization of the corporation. The bylaws include a listing of the powers of the board of directors, the shareholders, details on giving notice for and keeping records of meetings and decision, and instructions on the consequences of dissolution.

With a virtual corporation, there is no need for a separate set of bylaws. The operating agreement ought to be the primary and exclusive document for sorting out governance and finance within the corporation. The agreement should specify how notices are given for meetings, how meetings are conducted, the roles of the various players, and details about how to distribute profits, dur-

---

[5] VT. STAT. ANN. tit. 11A, §§ 6.01, 6.02.

[6] Vermont Secretary of State Corporations Division, http://www.sec.state.vt.us/corps/index.htm (last visited May 1, 2009).

ing good years; additional capital, as needed; and the remainders, upon dissolution.

Officers

The 2008 changes to the Vermont corporation code include elimination of the traditional prohibition against the same person serving as president and secretary of the corporation. Even in close corporations, this used to be a critical requirement—codifying a small hope that transparency and security would come if the person who recorded the actions of the corporation was not the person who made the decisions. But this restriction is gone now, the victim of doubt that it was ever very effective. The one-person corporation is now possible.

More likely, your virtual corporation will consist of a variety of individuals with various talents. Some of these individuals may choose to participate in management, and some may prefer to leave such matters to others. Those who accept responsibility should lead, but only with the trust and support of those who agree to follow.

If you choose not to appoint a board of directors, someone still must take charge of the details. You may call the person chief, leader, president, executive, or any other name that suits you. The operating agreement should direct how this person is appointed (and removed, if necessary), and articulate the person's powers. Because power corrupts, there should be someone else to oversee this chief's powers, holding the responsibility of questioning decisions. A fundamental rule of conflict avoidance is to separate the money from the power, thus justifying the selection of another separate player who keeps the finances. A further separation between the one who keeps the financial records and the one who writes the checks makes very good sense. Not that you are untrustworthy; but avoidance of temptation, or simply a reason to sleep more soundly at night knowing that the venture's funds are secure, is justification enough.

"Secretary" is the name given to the person who keeps the official records of a traditional corporation. Although the name does not matter, the function is critical—not just to keep the historical record clear but to ensure that future decisions are made with full awareness of what has come before. These records need not be hidden from anyone directly involved in the corporation. A secure web page where every set of minutes, all correspondence, contracts, and the current version of the operating agreement are kept demonstrates the openness of your venture and the sense that you are all in this endeavor together, as one body.

In a perfect democracy, officers are chosen for their skills and experience from among the entire membership. Positions of authority rotate at regular intervals, with each individual taking a turn at each position. But that is not a requirement. In fact, there are no requirements beyond the few details enunciated in the Vermont law. Your decision on how to organize your corporation will never be questioned by a Vermont official, because the operating agreement will remain proprietary. All Vermont has to know is the name of someone to contact in case there is a problem with filing of articles, amendments, or annual reports. Today the form for the articles requires a listing of a board of directors; when the virtual corporation forms are developed, that will be optional.

Meetings

Vermont law now defines "meeting" as "any structured communications conducted by participants in person or through use of electronic or telecommunications medium permitting simultaneous or sequentially structured communications for the purpose of reaching a collective agreement."[7] The boardroom, with its crystal pitchers and wrapped peppermints, may be converted to storage now. A meeting can be held from your desks, on the screen in front of you, via your voice picked up by a microphone, with all principals—wherever in the world they may be sitting—present and able to vote on a proposition. Meetings may even be held by asynchronous e-mail.

Meetings require notice. Traditionally, this was a letter, and later a fax, sent and received a set number of days before convening a meeting. The world has speeded up. Today, providing the rule is set forth in the operating agreement, notice may be given by voice mail, e-mail, fax, or other means, within minutes. There is no need to wait.

Traditionally, annual meetings and special meetings differ in the kind of notice required, with specific action agendas required to be included in the warning for special meetings. But agendas

[7] Vt. Stat. Ann. tit. 11, § 3001 (26).

for all meetings are well advised; while not mandated by law, they avoid surprises and relieve anxieties of those who may prefer not to participate, knowing that subjects of critical interest are not on the table.

Minutes of all meetings are kept to preserve a record of what has been done. There is no statutory minimum requirement for what minutes should contain. At least they should report the names and associations of those who are "present," list all motions (whether they are voted on or not), amendments, and votes. Listing every comment is excessive, but a good test of competent minutes is for those not present to know what happened, and why, without further inquiry.

Those who were present must approve all minutes. This process is essential to ensuring a full record exists of all action taken. The whole point is the instilling of confidence in those with whom the corporation deals. Good minutes reflect the discipline and order of the association.

Stock or Other Indicia of Ownership and Control

The operating agreement might create a system of awarding points to participants in the virtual corporation based on a majority shareholder decision of their contributions to the venture. This allocation might best be made after a short period of experience following incorporation, with regular opportunities to revisit, and award new points for active participants.

Future services may be pledged in exchange for stock, which would be escrowed until the services are provided.[8]

The determination of the value of such shares no longer must be included in the articles of incorporation. If there are different classes of shares, however, the differences must be included in the articles.[9]

Record Keeping

Retrievability is the minimum requirement for record keeping in the new virtual world. If you can print it out, all records may be kept electronically.[10]

[8] Vt. Stat. Ann. tit. 11A, § 6.21.

[9] Vt. Stat. Ann. tit. 11A, § 601(d).

[10] Vt. Stat. Ann. tit. 11, §§ 3026(f), 3058(c).

The Hosting Company

Although this information is never mentioned in the Vermont corporation law, the virtual corporation may be organized through services provided by a hosting company. The hosting company must be situated in Vermont and capable of providing entrepreneurs with the basic models for developing the virtual corporation and providing services that could include maintenance of finances and the keeping of records.

Arbitration

Conflicts distract businesses from business. Their swift resolution justifies including the requirement that all disputes between shareholders be addressed by binding arbitration. Vermont law requires explicit acknowledgement of the inclusion of arbitration requirements in the agreement by each of the signers of the document, displayed prominently (and usually included in separate paragraphs for each signer at the end of the agreement). Vermont law even specifies a form for such acknowledgements, without which arbitration is unenforceable, should a conflict arise.[11]

Conflicts of Interest

The new Vermont law establishes a new standard for determining conflicts. What is "fair to the corporation" is now the rule, meaning that a transaction between a shareholder and the corporation must be "comparable to an arm's length transaction, given the consideration paid or received by the corporation."[12]

The stigma of self-dealing is neutralized when operating agreements are specific on this subject. Vermont law intrudes in this area by defining a "material financial transaction" as one that "could reasonably be expected to impair the objectivity of the director's judgment."[13] In such cases, the law requires the affected director to leave the room (or in the Internet context, log off) for the remaining directors to make the decision free of any hint of coercion by the absent director.[14]

---

[11] VT. STAT. ANN. tit. 12, § 5652.
[12] VT. STAT. ANN. tit. 11A, § 8.60.
[13] VT. STAT. ANN. tit. 11A, § 8.60.
[14] VT. STAT. ANN. tit. 11A, § 8.62.

CHAPTER THREE

Post-Incorporation: Virtual Ethics and Corporate Responsibility in a Digital Era

If recent news and events are any yardsticks, lawyers face unprecedented pressure and exposure when it comes to advising corporate clients; and the virtual corporate client is no exception. Beyond start-up incorporation basics, corporate responsibility—also sometimes referred to as corporate social responsibility or responsible business—and related compliance and ethics issues must necessarily enter the lawyer's radar screen, especially when it comes to corporate operation, management or employee conduct, privacy and data management, and preservation of corporate brand.

Corporations today do not operate in a vacuum. Instead, with a gamut of exceptions, corporations are obligated to comply with an increasing body of statutory and regulatory frameworks. They are required to consider and take responsibility for their impact on a number of actors, including shareholders and customers, such as when their actions or lack of actions expose customers' sensitive data to the world. Even virtual corporations, created under the most flexible schemes, may find they are not insulated from traditional obligations.

With the legal creation of virtual corporations—that is, those as discussed in Chapter 1—comes an expanded role of the lawyer advocate, which may include advising clients on issues of ethics, transparency, and responsibility. Why? Because the virtual enterprise swings the door wide open when it comes to issues of risk and responsibility. And because virtual corporations will be born into a new corporate world that seeks to distance itself, whether by choice or by regulation, from practices associated with corporate irresponsibility. By virtue of the lack of physical "real world" presence, virtual companies may be vulnerable to unique, and some not-so-unique, risks and ensuing liability.

When it comes to responsibility and accountability today, there's much that corporations *do not have to do*—and when they do have to act, they are sometimes able to skate by, doing only what's minimally required. Yet, at any given moment, there are organizations *doing more*. As proof, momentarily redirect your iPhone, BlackBerry, or Netbook to Fortune's list of America's Best and Worst Companies for Social Responsibility.[1]

Corporate responsibility goes beyond trendy, however. It has long been "en vogue" and a core mission of progressive brick-and-mortar companies, such as Vermont's Ben & Jerry's and Seventh Generation, long before virtual corporations or virtual incorporation were ever conceived. Virtual corporations may very well up the ante of corporate responsibility, given today's corporate climate and the economic conditions into which virtual corporations are now being born.

While by no means comprehensive, this chapter serves as a foundation of basic ethical and corporate responsibility considerations lawyers will inevitably face as they advise virtual start-ups

[1] CNN.com, *America's Most Admired Companies, Best & Worst: Social Responsibility*, http://money.cnn.com/magazines/fortune/mostadmired/2008/best_worst/best4.html (last visited May 1, 2009).

interested in cutting-edge corporate forms, like Vermont's digital LLC, as well as traditional companies looking to move their businesses into a technology-driven medium or better position their businesses for today's and tomorrow's markets.

Social Corporate Responsibility Defined

Virtual corporations formed via the latest legal tools in business formation may be surprised to discover that their corporate activities impinge on questions of ethics or even morality, resulting in voluntary or discretionary modification of business practices.[2] Recognizing that they are a "different, highly flexible, beast," from the start, some virtual corporations may bask in their distinction by adopting business practices that reflect a progressive stance and visible commitment to more than the bottom line.

According to Philip Kotler and Nancy Lee, authors of *Corporate Social Responsibility: Doing the Most Good for Your Company and Your Cause,* "corporate social responsibility is a commitment to improve community well-being through discretionary business practices and contributions of corporate resources."[3] But corporate social responsibility extends beyond doing "good" by way of charitable giving to community initiatives, though that is what often comes to mind. It's a concept that reflects conscious business practices that "consider the interests of society by taking responsibility for the impact of their activities on customers, employees, shareholders, communities and the environment in all aspects of their operations."[4] Corporate social responsibility also includes thoughtful business practices that reflect integrity and fairness, while considering "internal stakeholder issues such as product quality, customer satisfaction, employee wages and benefits, and local community and environmental responsibilities," and maintaining regard for accountability.[5]

---

[2] PHILIP KOTLER & NANCY LEE, CORPORATE SOCIAL RESPONSIBILITY: DOING THE MOST GOOD FOR YOUR COMPANY AND YOUR CAUSE 3 (Wiley 2005).

[3] PHILIP KOTLER & NANCY LEE, *supra* note 2.

[4] Corporate Social Responsibility, http://discover.theiet.org/groups/Corporate%20Social%20Responsibility/tags/myspace (last visited May 1, 2009).

[5] Corporate Governance, http://www.corpgov.net/forums/commentary/entinel.html (last visited May 1, 2009).

An Ethical Foundation: The Virtual Corporation Mission Statement

A mission statement (or guiding principle) that outlines strategic vision and approach may go a long way toward the goals of social responsibility and transparency, and can prove helpful in supporting the virtual corporation's broader goals from the ground up. A mission statement can provide direction and a reference point for reevaluation as the virtual corporation grows and evolves, or when seemingly no longer applicable.

Protection of Critical Business Assets: Data and Intellectual Property

Whether your client's new company is virtual in the purest of forms, exists only in Second Life, or is a hybrid with an online and off-line presence, that company's information is a critical business asset that requires specific data protection efforts to ensure the "confidentiality, integrity and availability"[6] of that information.

By nature, virtual corporations may have heightened interest in protecting information, since data (i.e., intellectual property stored as electronic information) is the bedrock of their existence and operation. Simply put, without the data, they may cease to exist. While a traditional company may have a server room and backup tapes to store and restore data, as needed, the virtual corporation may lack such centralization or redundancy and may even depend on third parties with products designed for small or flexible businesses, such as virtual backup companies like Box.net or Mozy. While a traditional company may have filing cabinets overflowing with years of paper records (hard copies) containing work product or client information, or contacts on Rolodexes that could ensure business continuity, a virtual corporation may have none.

[6] Confidentiality, Integrity, and Availability, referred to as C.I.A. Triad, are the core principles of information security. *See* Information Security, http://en.wikipedia.org/wiki/CIA_Triad#Key_concepts (last visited May 1, 2009).

A Question of Responsibility: What Are Data and Access to That Data Worth to Your Client?

Virtual corporations that depend primarily on technology to function should contemplate what that data and access to that data are worth in terms of business continuity. For example, what would it mean to your client if she sat down one morning and her computer didn't work? Would revenue be lost? Would it have been worth it financially (factoring litigation risk into the equation) to have backed up that data elsewhere?

Protection of information as a business asset, as well as any corporate intellectual property or proprietary data, can be facilitated via the creation of policy and procedures, including a comprehensive *Risk Management Plan.* Even lawyers lacking technical backgrounds can help encourage new corporate clients to think about data as critical business assets and identify ways to evaluate threats and manage risk. While lawyers may necessarily help identify what, if any, legal obligations attach to a corporation (e.g., SOX, HIPAA, data breach notification laws), they can also help illuminate where the law leaves off (this alone may prove valuable, since it may help clients identify, assess, and manage risk) and help clients plan a risk management strategy.

Risk Management Plan: A Process Relevant to Virtual Start-Ups and New Businesses

In the context of data, risk management is defined as "the process of identifying vulnerabilities and threats to the information resources used by an organization in achieving business objectives, and deciding what countermeasures, if any, to take in reducing risk to an acceptable level, based on the value of the information resource to the organization."[7]

Businesses that gravitate to new business forms, such as Vermont's digital LLC/virtual incorporation, may be information intensive by nature. Accordingly, the management and security of that information is likely critical to business continuity and long-term success.

---

[7] ISACA (2006), *CISA Review Manual 2006*, http://en.wikipedia.org/wiki/Information_security#cite_note-2 (last visited May 1, 2009).

> When it comes to data and risk management, your virtual company client's stomach for risk and budget may aggressively drive its risk management and data security approach. A Risk Management Plan is foundational.

While virtual enterprises may have a vested interest in protecting data, they may also have legal obligations to protect information—namely sensitive personal information (e.g., customer, financial, or medical data)—as per data protection legal frameworks included in data breach prevention laws. Even when the reasons for protecting information center on legal compliance, virtual clients may have other reasons to be interested in (or perhaps should be interested in) the voluntary aspects of data protection, including remediation costs associated with data loss or breach, return on investment, negative public relations, and avoiding damage to reputation or brand.[8]

Companies that invest in safeguarding their information resources and, by extension, customer or client data, can gain consumer confidence and loyalty. When virtual companies are geographically dispersed and without a visible, physical brick-and-mortar address, the bar may be set even higher to secure and maintain confidence and loyalty and to establish credibility.

Data Protection Compliance and Encryption

Recently, states have begun to enact legislation that expands the focus on data breach notification to data containment by way of explicit compliance requirements for the protection of personal information (e.g., customer data). Nevada and Massachusetts are two trendsetting states that have recently set new regulations affecting the way organizations control and transmit sensitive data; and more states are surely following on their heels, including California.[9] These states impose tough requirements pertaining to

[8] Information Week, *Data Loss Costing Companies $6.6 Million Per Breach*, http://www.informationweek.com/news/security/attacks/showArticle.jhtml?articleID=213000512&subSection=News (Feb. 3, 2009) (noting that the "total average cost of a data breach [in 2008] reach $202 per record, a 2.5% increase since 2007").

[9] ITBusinessEdge, *California Lawmaker Wants Details in Breach Notifications*, http://www.itbusinessedge.com/cm/community/news/gov/blog/california-lawmaker-wants-details-in-breach-notifications/?cs=30974 (last visited May 1, 2009).

mandatory encryption of customer or resident data. For example, Massachusetts calls for the encryption of all portable personal information about residents, as well as the creation of comprehensive data security policy.[10]

Lawyers should be prepared to advise virtual corporate clients on the applicability of data protection and data breach regulation, particularly when their virtual client conducts business in jurisdictions with data protection laws or heightened requirements. While technology and technical requirements may seem intimidating conceptually, lawyers do not necessarily need technical mastery to advise virtual corporate clients of the legal importance of staying abreast of technology and industry trends where data is at the core of their business. The key is for virtual companies, like traditional companies, to follow—if not lead—the technology current. That includes keeping up to date on legal-technology-focused developments that may impact business and budgeting for Information Technology and Information Security, even if that means outsourcing to a third party.

Conscious data protection efforts—such as encrypting data in order to stay a step ahead in the legal and technology games, even when not legally required to do so, and proactively managing data risk—ultimately reflect thoughtful and socially responsible business practices and demonstrate awareness of emerging technology and security trends. This diligence may benefit the corporation later in defensive litigation, or even generally through a reputation for proactive and responsible business practices.

Checklist: Seven "Corporate Conscious" Data Risk Management Documents for Virtual Corporations

After your client has official legal entity status, it's time to contemplate the drafting of additional tools to ensure compliance and accountability, and to protect that entity and its goals, even when no legal requirements to do so exist. Here are seven corporate-conscious documents for start-ups and new businesses to consider drafting.

1. *Acceptable Use Policy (AUP).* Outlines ways in which networks, computers, phones, PDAs, or websites may be used (e.g., acceptable Internet use policy). Part and parcel to data security and protection

---

[10] *Businesses Protest Massachusetts Encryption Law,* http://www.theemailadmin.com/2009/01/businesses-protest-massachusetts-encryption-law/ (Jan. 22, 2009).

policy. Useful to have one for website services and one for company resources for employees.

2. *Privacy Policy.* Outlines how data is collected (e.g., use of website-enabled cookies or tracking software), used, and disclosed, as well as applicable security measures to protect that information.
3. *Comprehensive Risk Management Plan/Data Protection Policy.* Establishes control and accountability by documenting how and what you are going to protect.
4. *Internal Procedures.* Define the ground rules for protecting data and for carrying out policies. Formalize steps used for critical processes that must be done reliably.
5. *Incident Response Plan.* Guides the process for containing and remediating data leakage, data loss, data breaches (e.g., how to handle a website defacement, virus on your computer, loss of a laptop with client information).
6. *Disaster Recovery Plan.* Guides the process related to restoring business or recovering from disaster (e.g., fire, flood, theft of critical equipment, natural disaster).
7. *Electronic Data Retention Policy.* Outlines the logistics of data storage and retention (e.g., what data is retained and how long data will be retained before it's deleted), which may prove useful should the company encounter litigation/e-discovery.

Data Policy, Standards, and Guidelines: How to Help Virtual Company Clients Spot the Difference and Draft the Documents They Need

To help clients distinguish between data policy, standards, and guidelines, The SANS Institute, a leading authority on data security, explains:

> A policy is typically a document that outlines specific requirements or rules that must be met. In the information/network security realm, policies are usually point-specific, covering a single area. For example, an "Acceptable Use" policy would cover the rules and regulations for appropriate use of the computing facilities.
>
> A standard is typically collections of system-specific or procedural-specific requirements that must be met by everyone. . . .

A guideline is typically a collection of system specific or procedural specific "suggestions" for best practice. They are not requirements to be met, but are strongly recommended. Effective security policies make frequent references to standards and guidelines that exist within an organization.[11]

Note: Some organizations forego guidelines in favor of procedures where they want to be absolute about the steps in normal or critical processes.

Data Sharing and Management

For companies that exist solely online or operate by a geographically dispersed team (i.e., virtual team), issues of data sharing, transfer, and storage are uniquely distinct from traditional "offline" based companies (e.g., companies with central storage, either electronic and/or classic file cabinets). Virtual corporate clients will need to determine how to share information, transfer it, and store it—not only to ensure legal requirements are met (e.g., compliance to a law that requires encryption of transmitted personal data or data contained on portable—handheld—devices, like a BlackBerry), but as a matter of practicality, and ultimately, responsible corporate governance.

Virtual incorporation appreciates that in today's world, geography doesn't have to limit the team of employees a company can build, nor need it interfere with the sharing of data. With existing technology and services, such as ubiquitous applications like Google Apps (the suite of commercial grade Google collaborationt services), and ultramobile devices like the iPhone or BlackBerry, effective business communication across geographic boundaries is a reality for even end users who aren't technologically savvy.

With data sharing and management (and issues of transfer and storage) comes room for the virtual enterprise to entertain social responsibility. Beyond bandwidth, virtual enterprises may have to consider issues of information collection and storage, distant collaboration, access to information (particularly if that is confidential, proprietary, or sensitive—i.e., consumer—information), privacy, and data control.

[11] SANS Institute—The Sans Security Policy Project, http://www.sans.org/resources/policies/#name (last visited May 1, 2009).

Internet and Electronic-Mail Marketing

A lure of the online world is that it is incredibly easy to "appear big," especially on a small budget. Virtual corporations should be cognizant of ethical lines when it comes to communicating about their products to avoid false advertising or misleading consumers. While companies necessarily may have to cast their presence everywhere on the Internet (e.g., blogs, social networking sites, community forums), companies—virtual and off-line companies alike—should firmly keep in mind their brand, maintain consistency and professional appearance in all venues, and project that brand accordingly.

Virtual corporations should be aware of basic issues related to e-mail marketing, including spam (unsolicited, anonymously sent, bulk or mass mailing). With respect to bulk mail, companies should also observe accepted e-mail etiquette and customs; and they should ensure compliance with any applicable consumer opt-out notifications. Companies can also use an online e-mail marketing source with a good, established reputation to ensure compliance.

Virtual Corporations, Marketers, Spammers, Phishers, and Identity Thieves: Take Note of These Laws

Identity Theft Enforcement and Restitution Act of 2008 (H.R. 5983, signed by President Bush in Sept. 2008): This statute gives prosecutors ammunition to go after those who use "botnets" (i.e., networks of infected computers) to send spam, among other tools for combating cybercrime including cyber extortion.

CAN-SPAM Act of 2003 (Controlling the Assault of Non-Solicited Pornography and Marketing): Sets forth commercial e-mail requirements, establishes penalties, and provides a spam opt-out).

State Laws: Patchworks of laws exist related to Internet marketing, such as California's Anti-Phishing Laws.

Virtual corporations, and the lawyers advising them, who have interest in social responsibility should also be aware of website privacy issues including data collection and tracking. Many websites and services engage in tracking of site visitors (e.g., geographic location, IP address, time of visit, pages visited, computer name, host name, referring links), and a company may or may not be aware of the exact nature of the harvested or collected information.

Corporations should become familiar with applicable legal restrictions or implications of data collection, use of cookies, tokens, or other tracking software, spyware, or devices, even if the data may not seem "readable" or comprehensible to a nontechnical person. As a matter of social responsibility, which entails consideration for others beyond the corporation, virtual companies with a Web presence should consider conspicuous placement of a privacy policy on their site to notify users about what, if any, forms of data collection, tracking, or other monitoring occur.

Checklist: Basics for Creating a Corporate Website Privacy Policy

To help your virtual company client devise a website privacy policy, the following list contains several elements commonly found in online privacy policies:

1. Disclosure about what data is collected, how it is collected, and why it is collected (e.g., tracking, analysis). This disclosure may include reference to data logs (e.g., IP addresses, browser type, data/time stamps) and cookies (e.g., Session ID or persistent cookies, which are small files stored on a user's computer).
2. Explanation of efforts taken to protect data.
3. Disclosure about links to other sites (e.g., ones that take you beyond the origin site).
4. Explanation about what is done with collected data, particularly with respect to third parties. Is information sold or traded with third parties? Is it personally identifiable?
5. Explanation of how to opt out of receiving promotional mail, including e-newsletters or bulk e-mail.
6. Disclosure of rights related to changes to the privacy policy (e.g., reserving the right to amend the policy at any time).

Blogs

Blogging is revolutionizing the way companies reach audiences, and blogs are quickly becoming the ultimate tool in mass communication. A blog, or "web log," is a website that provides commentary, writings, or rants on a subject (think virtual diary).[12]

[12] Wikipedia, "Blog," http://en.wikipedia.org/wiki/Blog (last visited May 1, 2009).

Increasingly, companies are using blogs as a marketing or advertising tool to reach their target market.

Virtual corporations that utilize blogs (and social networks with embedded communication tools, such as blog feeds, micro-blogs) as a marketing tool necessarily must blog with caution, keeping in mind that blogs and the content therein may be used for litigation purposes and/or impact their brands. Given the electronic medium, corporations should also keep in mind that data lives in perpetuity. Even when deleted, data often can be resurrected, though the cost may be prohibitive. Of possibly even greater concern is that information posted on a blog can be easily copied and quickly disseminated across the Internet. In short, as soon as a blog entry is published, the blog author or company loses control over that information.

When it comes to employees, a virtual company may choose to look at blogging as a way employees communicate. But it also must be cognizant that whatever gets blogged—anonymously or not—about the company ultimately becomes a reflection of the company, whether they intended to create that impression or not. While they are incredibly powerful and effective in promoting a company, corporate blogs or employee blogs carry the further risk of being used to disseminate confidential or sensitive data, inadvertently or otherwise. Though companies should not be fearful of blogging, lawyers may discover they can assist companies in drafting corporate policies that address blogs.

Micro-Blogging: Another Corporate Policy Consideration

The emergence of micro-blogging (i.e., Twitter) which permits users to blog in a limited number of characters, by laptop or mobile device, should also cross the virtual company's radar policy screen.[13] With micro-blogging comes the possibility of instantaneous and viral sharing of information, which could magnify a company's successes and mistakes.

Social Media and Networks

Virtual corporations will discover that social networks are becoming increasingly important to marketing success. The traditional

[13] Wikipedia, "Micro-blogging," http://en.wikipedia.org/wiki/Micro-blogging (last visited May 1, 2009).

one-way marketing model is fading fast. Two-way, limitless discussion is moving in. As individuals and companies increasingly use social media (e.g., wikis, forums, podcasts) and networking sites (e.g., LinkedIn, Legal OnRamp, Flickr, Twitter) for effective business communication, social responsibility becomes an even more important concept. Given the viral nature of social networking, a company's brand or reputation can practically change overnight. What a company does or what it reveals in communication will be scrutinized online (e.g., a company should be prepared for unintended consequences or backlash, including unfavorable attention in social media).

Corporate Pro Bono

Traditional corporations have long participated in volunteer community activities and supported nonprofit missions. Even though virtual corporations may be primarily based in cyberspace, there is no reason they cannot continue charitable giving. Bloggers, for instance, have already embraced the giving spirit, posting donation "badges" (i.e., clickable banners or graphics) that allow visitors to contribute to causes or nonprofit organizations; and a growing number of online-based companies advertise donation of a percentage of profits to nonprofits. Other corporations have launched eco-initiatives, such as the baby gear recycling program developed by online retailer BabyEarth. Increasingly, corporations are discovering the "halo effect" of social corporate responsibility—that "Environmental and social performances are tangible business assets that complement financial performance."[14]

Employee and Management Conduct

One of the great things about virtual incorporation is that people can come together from all parts of the country or world to work on a single project. Take the writing of this book, for instance; its authors are spread out hundreds and even thousands of miles apart. When people come together to create a business in a decentralized fashion and without traditional oversight, it may prove useful to draft specific policies, beyond the operating agreement,

[14] Ken Reibel, *Why Should Companies Be Socially Responsible?* (Apr. 9, 2008), http://www.expressmilwaukee.com/article-1600-why-should-companies-be-socially-responsible.html (last visited May 1, 2009).

that outline expectations and address concerns unique to the corporation's nature—even though such documents might not otherwise be required or even relevant in a traditional corporation environment.

Second Life and Virtual Worlds

Virtual incorporation has the potential for broad online appeal, extending beyond what some may envision as the typical "virtual company" (e.g., an online version of a brick-and-mortar enterprise or dispersed collaboration) to possibly encompass corporations that "exist only in Second Life."[15] Even in these worlds, corporations need to be cognizant that by way of incorporation they are legal entities; and with that status comes obligations to transact business as they would off-line (i.e., legally and with concern for the implications of their business practices).

Domain Names

Virtual incorporation appears to open the possibility for individuals or organizations to register a domain name using the ".US" domain. To obtain the .US domain, registrants are required to comply with the U.S. Nexus Requirement for .US domains, which requires demonstration of a substantive connection to the United States.[16] One of the ways compliance is met is if the individual or organization can show that they are

> an entity or organization that is (i) incorporated within one of the fifty (50) U.S. states, the District of Columbia, or any of the United States possessions or territories or (ii) organized or otherwise constituted under the laws of a state of the United States of America, the District of Columbia or any of its possessions or territories.[17]

[15] Wagner James Au, *New World Newsfeed: The Era of the Virtual Company*, http://nwn.blogs.com/nwn/2008/06/new-world-new-4.html (last visited May 1, 2009).
[16] Neustar, *U.S. Nexus Requirement*, http://www.neustar.us/policies/nexus_requirement.html (last visited May 1, 2009).
[17] *Id.*

1. A natural person (i) who is a citizen or permanent resident of the United States of America or any of its possessions or territories, or (ii) whose primary place of domicile is in the United States of America or any of its possessions, or

While virtual incorporation may potentially allow expanded business via use of the .US domain, lawyers should be mindful that such use potentially incites ethical and legal complications (e.g., issues of jurisdiction, fraud, litigation costs) that otherwise might not have existed.

Moreover, companies should be aware that when they register a top-level domain (e.g., .COM), that same name could be registered using another top-level domain (e.g., .NET or .ORG). Accordingly, corporations may wish to register the same name with multiple top-level domains to prevent cybersquatting, confusion, or misdirection (e.g., Internet traffic or prospective customers going to the wrong address). The same holds true for spelling variations. Given that registering domain names is quite inexpensive, obtaining multiple registrations is probably worth the cost and peace of mind, at least in curbing future headaches.

Cyberethics

According to Symantec, a leading security applications vendor, "Cyber ethics is a code of behavior for using the Internet."[18] While the topic of cyberethics may seem most relevant to discussions between parents and children (e.g., homework and plagiarism, online stranger danger), online companies may find the discussion of cyberethics relevant to their corporate strategy, particularly depending on the nature of their business and its stance toward protecting children in the online medium. Take for instance, MySpace. In February 2009, the social networking site announced that it used cutting-edge technology to identify and remove 90,000 registered sex offenders from the site.[19] How a virtual company conducts business may impact the online landscape, for better or worse.

---

2. An entity or organization that is (i) incorporated within one of the fifty (50) U.S. states, the District of Columbia, or any of the United States possessions or territories or (ii) organized or otherwise constituted under the laws of a state of the United States of America, the District of Columbia or any of its possessions or territories, or

3. An entity or organization (including a federal, state, or local government of the United States, or a political subdivision thereof) that has a bona fide presence in the United States.

[18] Symantec Corporation, *Cyber Ethics*, http://www.symantec.com/norton/familyresources/resources.jsp?title=ar_cyber_ethics (last visited May 1, 2009).

[19] *MySpace, Facebook Spar over Family Safety*, http://news.cnet.com/8301-17939_109-10155596-2.html (Feb 3, 2009).

Does Your Client's Virtual Company Practice "Good" Cyberethics?

According to the Department of Justice, "The term 'cyberethics' refers to a code of safe and responsible behavior for the Internet Community. Cyberethics involves understanding the risks of harmful and illegal behavior online and learning how to protect ourselves, and other Internet users, from such behavior."[20]

Terrorism

As with any legal form of business, the possibility exists that virtual incorporation will be abused—namely, used for purposes of fraud, other illegal activities, or terrorism.[21] But corporate social responsibility has the potential to impact terrorism; and optimistically, virtual corporations that operate with social responsibility on the radar screen may be a counterweight (not to mention traditional legal tools and mechanism to combat threats). According to a post-9/11 survey of Fortune 1000 CEOs, research found that "global warming, the status of world communities, even support of terrorism can be affected by major corporations being attuned to issues of corporate social responsibility."[22] That same study found that "Fifty-two percent of Fortune 1000 CEOs said they think that corporations acting responsibly to communities around the world can ebb the support of terrorist groups."

As with any business, the virtual corporation has the potential to shape the larger community, for good or bad. To expand upon the earlier discussion about data security, virtual corporations that practice responsible computing and implement effective data security measures and keep their systems updated may actually prove useful in deterring computer-related crime or even cyberextortion and cyberterrorism.

[20] United States Department of Justice, Cybercrime & Intellectual Property Section, http://www.usdoj.gov/criminal/cybercrime/cyberethics.htm (last visited May 1, 2009).

[21] David Johnson, *Virtual Companies*, http://dotank.nyls.edu/june18virtualcorp.html (last visited May 1, 2009).

[22] Global Policy Forum, *CEOs Say Environment, World Communities, and Terrorism All Affected By Big Business*, http://www.globalpolicy.org/reform/business/2002/ceosurvey.htm (last visited May 1, 2009).

CHAPTER FOUR

Virtual Incorporation FAQs

Q: What Is a Virtual Company?

A: A virtual company is a template for the development of joint projects by previously unaffiliated individuals with common goals and ideas. It is designed to join these individuals together in a legal organization that fulfills their basic needs for structure without burdening them with bureaucratic or hierarchical modes of governance and that allows for the realization of their dreams, hopes, and promises.

Q: What Is "Virtual Incorporation"?

A: A virtual corporation is a legal idea manifested by a name, an official registration with a state corporations division, an operating agreement constituting a contract binding individuals in the performance of joint endeavors, and the active involvement of those participants for mutual inspiration and financial gain. A virtual incorporation has these elements: (1) the formation of a limited liability entity *without* the requirements of a physical location or address, (2) capitalization in the form of money or property contributed to the business, or a hierarchical management structure, and (3) *with* the ability to make electronic filings and engage in electronic communications for its corporate governance.

Q: How Does Vermont's Approach Revolutionize, If at All, the Way Online Start-Up Companies Are Formed or Operate?

A: Vermont gives limited liability protection to individuals or groups who seek to start a business or collaborate on a business venture or project. As Professor David Johnson, the force behind Vermont's effort, explains:

> Under traditional legal doctrines, those that style themselves as companies are at risk of being re-characterized as partnerships, losing any claim to limited liability. In most cases, they have to rely on an individual participant to hold and administer any company funds (try opening a bank account on behalf of a World of Warcraft guild! Don't count on a secure return on your scarce attention resources in Eve Online, the head of which declares "fraud is fun!"). Online groups lack reliable means of entering into contracts, as groups, with third parties. And they would have a hard time appearing in court to defend their rights.[1]

Q: Where Does the Virtual Company Exist or Conduct Business?

A: The virtual company exists in the ether, and in the plans and products produced by its participants. It conducts its business by Internet. It is paperless, pragmatic, and leaves no carbon footprint.

Q: Do I Need a "Technical" Background in Order to Advise a Virtual Company Client or Understand Virtual Incorporation?

A: You need to know how the law works, and how to focus the dreams of creative people into practical, realistic, and understandable commitments. You do not need to be a geek yourself. Leave the noodling to the geniuses. Trust is essential in any relationship, particularly one based on ideas, where participants seldom meet except on a screen and products are created in code.

[1] David Johnson, Virtual Companies, http://dotank.nyls.edu/june18virtualcorp.html (last visited May 1, 2009).

Q: Can a Traditional Company Take Advantage of the Digital LLC Form?

A: The new Vermont law's advantages are not limited purely to virtual corporations. The electronic filing and record keeping are available now for any corporation or LLC organized under Vermont law.

Q: Don't Other States Offer Comparable Formation Options?

A: What separates Vermont from other states, at least at present, is the freedom the new law allows from traditional statutory restraints on how business is conducted. Vermont is the first jurisdiction to embrace the Net fully, respecting the integrity of electronic media and the possibilities inherent in corporate organization without a formal presence in the state beyond a registered agent.

Q: What Are the Advantages of Virtual Incorporation?

A: Virtual incorporation affords its contributors the freedom and flexibility to operate their business without the traditional constraints of physicality, formality, and hierarchy. For businesses that lend themselves to many varying levels of contributors and that want to incentivize the group of contributors as a whole, virtual incorporation provides the mechanism for this operation, while still retaining the limited liability protection of a traditional corporation.

Q: How Do I Determine Whether Virtual Incorporation Is the Right Option for My Client?

A: Try one on for size. Consider the possibilities of inventing organizational structures and operating agreements that are limited only by the imagination of the participants. Celebrate the release of creativity from the prison of formality and hierarchy. This is not your father's corporation. It is an experiment in the expression of the spirit, unburdened by formulaic restrictions. Not everyone is ready for this form. Some need the safety and security of tradition, the restraint of resolutions neatly stacked and copied, the stale odor of the boardroom, the impression left by the official seal. But a corporation is only an idea. It isn't a set of forms, minutes, and other official chaff, stuck on a shelf. It is a way of bringing people together for mutual benefit. Its prize is limited liability and the protection of assets. That is society's consideration for your industry and your commitment.

The argument against the Amazon Kindle, the Sony Reader, and other devices that present text in electronic form is the loss of the tactile sensations of the book itself, the crisp pages, cracking spine, hard board jacket. But when you read a good book, you leave the page behind. You leave the room and enter a different plane of consciousness, into which only the most annoying sounds or people can intrude. The virtual corporation represents the same transformative experience, without the interruptions.

CHAPTER FIVE

Business Formation Resources for Lawyers and "Virtual" Clients

Secretary of State Listings—State by State

Alabama Secretary of State

P.O. Box 5616
Montgomery, AL 36103-5616
Ph: 334-242-7200
http://www.sos.state.al.us

Alaska Division of Corporations

P.O. Box 110806
333 Willoughby Avenue, 9th Floor
Juneau, AK 99811-0808
Ph: 907-465-2550
http://www.commerce.state.ak.us/occ

Arizona Secretary of State

1700 West Washington Street, 7th Floor
Phoenix, AZ 85007-2888
Ph: 520-628-6583
http://www.azsos.gov

Arkansas Secretary of State

State Capitol, RM 256
Little Rock, AR 72201
Ph: 501-682-1010
http://www.sos.arkansas.gov

California Secretary of State

1500 11th Street
Sacramento, California 95814
Ph: 916-653-6814
http://www.sos.ca.gov

Colorado Department of State

Suite 200
1700 Broadway, Denver, CO 80290
Ph: 303-894-2200
http://www.sos.state.co.us

Connecticut Secretary of the State

ATTN: Capitol Office
P.O. Box 150470
Hartford, CT 06115-0470
Ph: 860-509-6212
http://www.sots.ct.gov

Delaware Division of Corporations

P.O. Box 898
Dover, DE 19903
Ph: 302-739-3073
http://corp.delaware.gov

Office of the Secretary of the District of Columbia

1350 Pennsylvania Ave., NW, Room 419
Washington, DC 20004
Ph: 202-727-6306
http://os.dc.gov

Florida Department of State

Division of Corporations
Clifton Building
2661 Executive Center Circle
Tallahassee, FL 32301
Ph: 850-245-6500
http://www.dos.state.fl.us

Georgia Secretary of State

Corporations Division
2 MLK Jr. Dr. S.E.
Suite 315, West Tower
Atlanta, Georgia 30334
Ph: 404-656-2817
http://sos.georgia.gov

Hawaii Department of Commerce and Consumer Affairs

P.O. Box 40
Honolulu, HI 96810
Ph: 808-586-2744
http://hawaii.gov/dcca/areas/breg

Idaho Office of the Secretary of State

P.O. Box 83720
Boise ID 83720-0080
Ph: 208-334-2300
http://www.idsos.state.id.us

Illinois Secretary of State

Business Services
69 W. Washington
Suite 1240
Chicago, IL 60602
Ph: 312-793-3380
http://www.cyberdriveillinois.com

Indiana Secretary of State

201 Statehouse
Indianapolis, IN 46204
Ph: 317-232-6531
http://www.in.gov/sos

Iowa Secretary of State

First Floor, Lucas Building
321 E. 12th St.
Des Moines, IA 50319
Ph: 515-281-5204
http://www.sos.state.ia.us

Kansas Secretary of State

Memorial Hall, 1st Floor
120 SW 10th Avenue
Topeka, KS 66612-1594
Ph: 785-296-4564
http://www.kssos.org

Kentucky Office of the Secretary of State

The Capitol Building
700 Capital Avenue
Suite 152
Frankfort, KY 40601
Ph: 502-564-3490
http://www.sos.ky.gov

Louisiana Secretary of State

P.O. Box 94125
Baton Rouge, LA 70804-9125
Ph: 225-922-1000
http://www.sos.louisiana.gov

Maine Department of the Secretary of State

Bureau of Corporation, Elections and Commissions
101 State House Station
Augusta, Maine 04333-0101
Ph: 207-624-7735
http://maine.gov/sos

Maryland Office of the Secretary of State

16 Francis Street
Annapolis, MD 21401
Ph: 410-974-5521
http://www.sos.state.md.us

Massachusetts Secretary of the Commonwealth

One Ashburton Place, 17th floor
Boston, MA 02108
Ph: 617-727-9640
http://www.sec.state.ma.us

Michigan Department of State

Corporation Division
P.O. Box 30054
Lansing, MI 48909
Ph: 517-241-6470
http://www.michigan.gov/sos

Minnesota Office of the Secretary of State

Retirement Systems of Minnesota Building
60 Empire Drive, Suite 100
St Paul, MN 55103
Ph: 651-296-2803
http://www.sos.state.mn.us

Mississippi Secretary of State

401 Mississippi Street
Jackson, MS 39201
Ph: 601-359-1350
http://www.sos.state.ms.us

Missouri Office of the Secretary of State

State Capitol, Room 208
State Information Center, 600 W. Main
Jefferson City, MO 65101
Ph: 573-751-4936
http://www.sos.mo.gov

Montana Secretary of State

P.O. Box 202801
Helena, MT 59620-2801
Ph: 406-444-2034
http://sos.mt.gov

Nebraska Secretary of State

State Capitol, Suite 2300
P.O. Box 94608
Lincoln, NE 68509-4608
Ph: 402-471-2554
http://www.sos.state.ne.us

Nevada Secretary of State

Nevada State Capitol Building
101 North Carson Street, Suite 3
Carson City, NV 89701
Ph: 775-684-5708
http://sos.state.nv.us

New Hampshire Department of State

State House, Room 204
Concord, NH 03301
Ph: 603-271-3242
http://www.sos.nh.gov

State of New Jersey Department of State

P.O. Box 308
Trenton, NJ 08625
Ph: 609-292-9292
http://www.state.nj.us/state

New Mexico Secretary of State

New Mexico State Capitol
325 Don Gaspar, Suite 300
Santa Fe, NM 87503
Ph: 505-827-3600
http://www.sos.state.nm.us

New York Department of State

Department of State
One Commerce Plaza
99 Washington Avenue
Albany, NY 12231-0001
Ph: 518-474-4752
http://www.dos.state.ny.us

North Carolina Department of the Secretary of State

Corporations Division
P.O. Box 29622
Raleigh, NC 27626-0622
Ph: 919-807-2225
http://www.secretary.state.nc.us

North Dakota Secretary of State

State of North Dakota
600 E. Boulevard Ave, Dept 108, 1st Floor
Bismarck, ND 58505-0500
Ph: 701-328-2900
http://www.nd.gov/sos

Ohio Secretary of State

180 East Broad Street
Columbus, OH 43215
Ph: 614-466-2655
http://www.sos.state.oh.us

Oklahoma Secretary of State

2300 N. Lincoln Blvd., Suite 101
Oklahoma City, OK 73105-4897
Ph: 405-521-3912
http://www.sos.state.ok.us

Oregon Secretary of State

136 State Capitol
Salem, OR 97301
Ph: 717-787-1057
http://www.sos.state.or.us

Pennsylvania Department of State

Corporation Bureau
206 North Office Building
Harrisburg, PA 17120
Ph: 717-787-1057
http://www.dos.state.pa.us

Rhode Island Office of the Secretary of State

82 Smith Street
State House Room 217
Providence, RI 02903
Ph: 401-222-2357
http://www.sec.state.ri.us

South Carolina Secretary of State

P.O. Box 11350
Columbia, SC 29211
Ph: 803-734-2158
http://www.scsos.com

South Dakota Secretary of State

Capitol Building
500 East Capitol Ave, Suite 204
Pierre, SD 57501-5070
Ph: 605-773-3537
http://www.sdsos.gov

Tennessee Department of State

312 Rosa L. Parks Avenue
6th Floor, Snodgrass Tower
Nashville, TN 37243-1102
Ph: 615-741-2286
http://www.state.tn.us/sos

Texas Secretary of State

P.O. Box 12887
Austin, TX 78711-2887
Ph: 512-463-5555
http://www.sos.state.tx.us

Utah Division of Corporation and Commercial Code

160 East 300 South 2nd Floor
Salt Lake City, UT 84111
Ph: 801-530-4849
http://corporations.utah.gov/

Vermont Secretary of State

26 Terrace Street
Montpelier, VT 05609-1101
Ph: 802-828-2363 or 800-439-8683
http://www.sec.state.vt.us

Secretary of the Commonwealth of Virginia

P.O. Box 2454
Richmond, VA 23218
Ph: 804-786-2441
http://www.soc.state.va.us

Washington Secretary of State

P.O. Box 40220
Olympia, WA 98504-0220
Ph: 360-902-4151
http://www.secstate.wa.gov

West Virginia Secretary of State

Bldg. 1, Suite 157-K
1900 Kanawha Blvd. East
Charleston, WV 25305-0770
Ph: 304-558-8000
http://www.wvsos.com

Wisconsin Office of the Secretary of State

The Office of the Secretary of State
P.O. Box 7848
Madison, WI 53707-7848
Ph: 608-266-8888
http://www.sos.state.wi.us

Wyoming Secretary of State

The Capitol Building
200 West 24th Street, Cheyenne, WY 82002
Ph: 307-777-7378
http://soswy.state.wy.us

Attorney Bar Resources

American Bar Association—Blawg Directory

Directory of legal blogs, including corporate law and business formation blogs
http://abajournal.com/blawgs

American Bar Association—Section of Business Law

Cutting-edge resources for lawyers looking to meet needs of their business clients
http://www.abanet.org/buslaw/home.shtml

American Bar Association—Section of Science and Technology

Provides up-to-date substantive technology practice resources
http://www.abanet.org/scitech

Start-Up Resources

American Management Association

Offers seminars and resources for corporations, small businesses, and solo entrepreneurs
http://www.amanet.org

Entrepreneur.com

Online resource for the start-up business
http://www.entrepreneur.com

Inc.

"The Daily Resource for Entrepreneurs"
http://www.inc.com

SCORE

Offers free and confidential business advice to entrepreneurs
http://www.score.org/index.html

Website/Blog Launch Tools

Blogger

http://www.blogger.com

GoDaddy

https://www.godaddy.com

Official website for .US (domain)

http://www.nic.us

TypePad

http://www.typepad.com

Wordpress

http://wordpress.org
http://wordpress.com

Social Networking/Online Virtual Company Communication

Big Tent

A free, easy-to-use tool for communicating and organizing online and in-person groups
https://www.bigtent.com

Facebook

A tool to connect and communicate with people and businesses
http://www.facebook.com

FriendFeed

A tool that creates a customized feed of collaborative sites.
http://friendfeed.com

Legal OnRamp

An online "collaboration system" for lawyers and third-party service providers
http://www.legalonramp.com

LinkedIn

An online networking and relationship-building tool
http://www.linkedin.com

MySpace

A community for online information exchange and communication
http://www.myspace.com

Twitter

Micro-blogging, communication service that allows quick communication
http://twitter.com

Instant Communication/Geographically Dispersed Communication Tools

AIM (AOL Instant Messenger)

http://dashboard.aim.com/aim

Google Chat

http://www.google.com/talk

MSN Web Messenger

http://webmessenger.msn.com

Skype

http://www.skype.com

Yahoo! Messenger

http://messenger.yahoo.com

Virtual Collaboration Tools/Software

Buzzword

"The First Real Word Processor for the Web," which allows users to invite others to collaborate
https://buzzword.acrobat.com

Google Docs (Apps)

A web-based word processor and spreadsheet suite that offers shared user access
http://docs.google.com

PBWorks

Offers hosted collaboration solutions
http://pbworks.com

Wikispaces

Offers web site space for collaboration
http://www.wikispaces.com/

Information Security Resources

Federal Trade Commission

Protecting Personal Information, A Guide for Businesses
http://www.ftc.gov/bcp/conline/edcams/infosecurity/index.html

National Institute of Standards and Technology (NIST)

Computer Security Resource Center
http://csrc.nist.gov

SANS Institute

Information security training, leadership, and research resource
http://www.sans.org

State Security Breach Notification Laws

National Conference of State Legislatures; maintains a list of breach notification laws
http://www.ncsl.org/programs/lis/cip/priv/breachlaws.htm

Social Responsibility

Tim Sanders, *Saving the World at Work: What Companies and Individuals Can Do to Go Beyond Making a Profit to Making a Difference* (Broadway Business, 2008).

Virtual Companies

Virtual Companies

An evolving resource site related to Vermont Virtual Companies
http://vermontvirtual.org/Main_Page

Do Tank and the Democracy Design Workshop

Describes the Vermont Virtual Company Project
http://dotank.nyls.edu/VisualCorporation.html

Virtual Mailing Addresses

Earth Class Mail

http://www.earthclassmail.com

Virtual Worlds/Virtual Business Meetings

Benjamin Tyson Duranske, *Virtual Law: Navigating the Legal Landscape of Virtual Worlds* (American Bar Association, 2008).

Second Life

A 3-D virtual world (think, digital real world)
http://secondlife.com

Virtual Worlds Review

Provides links to virtual worlds
http://www.virtualworldsreview.com

APPENDIX A

Amendments to Vermont Legislation to Create "Virtual Incorporation"

From No. 190, An Act Relating to Miscellaneous Tax Amendments, effective July 1, 2008*

Sec. 1. 11 V.S.A. § 3001 is amended to read:
§ 3001. DEFINITIONS

As used in this chapter:

* * *

(15) "Operating agreement" means ~~the agreement in writing~~ any form of description of membership rights and obligations

*Initially introduced H.0458, An Act Relating to Digital Corporate Transactions, became part of H.0888, An Act Relating to Miscellaneous Tax Amendments (2007–08 Legislative Session), which is outlined here in relevant part. The Vermont Secretary of State Web Site explains Title 11 Section 3001 Digital Corps/LLC:

under section 3003 of this title, stored or depicted in any tangible or electronic medium, which is agreed to by the members, including amendments to the agreement.

* * *

(19) "Signed" includes any symbol or electronic schema that may be prescribed by the secretary of state that is executed or adopted by a person with the present intention to authenticate a record.

* * *

(23) "Document" means information that is inscribed on a tangible medium or that is stored in an electronic or other medium and is retrievable in perceivable form.

(24) "Writing" means written communications, including letters, faxes, e-mails, or other electronic formats that may be prescribed by the secretary of state.

(25) "Delivery" means surface mail or methods of electronic transmission the secretary of state may prescribe.

(26) "Meeting" means any structured communications conducted by participants in person or through the use of electronic or telecommunications medium permitting simultaneous or sequentially structured communications for the purpose of reaching a collective agreement.

Sec. 2. 11 V.S.A. § 3026(f) is added to read:

(f) An original copy may consist of an electronic communication received by the secretary of state's office, endorsement may consist of an attached electronic record, and the delivery of a duplicate may be done electronically.

Sec. 3. 11 V.S.A. § 3058(c) is amended to read:

(c) A company may maintain its records in other than written form if such form is capable of conversion into written form

---

This Act allows the company and their participants to dictate almost all of the terms of their internal organizational and operational communications between them by means of a digital operating agreement—thus dispensing with the standard paper-based format. Participants are free to agree upon the terms of their relationship, and how the company is to be governed, the economic relationships between them, how meetings are to be conducted, and other internal matters. Vermont Secretary of State, Corporations Division, http://www.sec.state.vt.us/corps/corpindex.htm (last visited June 10, 2009).

within a reasonable time or into an electronic form that may be prescribed by the secretary of state.

Sec. 4. 11A V.S.A. § 1.20 is amended to read:
§ 1.20. FILING REQUIREMENTS

* * *

(d) The document must be typewritten or printed or, if electronically transmitted, it must be in a format that can be retrieved or reproduced in typewritten or printed form or in an electronic format prescribed by the secretary of state.

* * *

(h) If the secretary of state has prescribed a mandatory form or electronic format for the document under section 1.21 of this title, the document must be in or on the prescribed form.

* * *

(j)(1) Any of the terms of a plan or filed documents may be made dependent on facts ascertainable outside the plan or filed documents as follows:

(A) The manner in which the facts operate on the terms of the plan or filed document must be clearly and expressly set forth in the plan or filed document.

(B) The facts may include without limitation actions or events within the control of, or determinations made by, a party to the plan or filing the filed document or a representative of a party to the plan or filing the filed document.

(2) As used in this section:

(A) "Filed document" means a document filed with the secretary of state under any provision of this title, except chapter 15 or section 16.22 of this title.

(B) "Plan" means a plan of merger or share exchange.

Sec. 5. 11A V.S.A. § 1.21(a) is amended to read:

(a) The secretary of state may prescribe the form or electronic format of and furnish on request forms or specifications for formats for:

(1) articles of incorporation. such form shall note the information required under subsection 2.02(a) of this title, together with a summary of such information or provisions as are permitted by this title;

(2) an application for a certificate of good standing;

(3) a foreign corporation's application for a certificate of authority to transact business in this state;

(4) a foreign corporation's application for a certificate of withdrawal; and

(5) the annual report.

Sec. 6. 11A V.S.A. § 1.23(a) is amended to read:

§ 1.23. EFFECTIVE TIME AND DATE OF DOCUMENT

(a) Except as provided in subsection (b) of this section, ~~section~~ subsection 1.24(c) of this title, and section 2.03 of this title, a document accepted for filing is effective ~~at the time of filing on the date it is filed, as evidenced by the secretary of state's date and time endorsement on the original document~~:

(1) at the date and time of filing, as evidenced by such means as the secretary of state may use for the purpose of recording the date and time of filing; or

(2) at the time specified in the document as its effective time on the date it is filed.

Sec. 7. 11A V.S.A § 1.24(a) is amended to read:

(a) A domestic or foreign corporation may correct a document filed by the secretary of state if the document:

(1) is incomplete;

(2) contains an incorrect statement; or

(3) was defectively executed, attested, sealed, verified, or acknowledged; or

(4) the electronic transmission of which was defective.

Sec. 8. 11A V.S.A. § 1.25(b) is amended to read:

(b) The secretary of state files a document by ~~stamping or otherwise endorsing~~ recording it as "Filed" together with his or her name and official title ~~and~~ on the date and time of receipt, on both the ~~original and the document copy~~ document and on the record of the receipt for the filing fee. After filing a document, except as provided in sections 5.03 and 15.10 of this title, the secretary of state shall deliver a copy of the document ~~copy, with the~~ and filing fee receipt (or acknowledgement of receipt if no fee is required) ~~attached,~~ to the domestic or foreign corporation or its representative.

Sec. 9. 11A V.S.A. § 1.27 is amended to read:

§ 1.27. EVIDENTIARY EFFECT OF COPY OF FILED DOCUMENT

~~(a) A certificate attached to a copy of a document filed by the secretary of state, bearing his or her signature (which may be in~~

~~facsimile) and the seal of this state, is conclusive evidence that the original document is on file with the secretary of state.~~

~~(b) A certificate by the secretary of state that a diligent search has failed to locate documents claimed to be filed with the secretary of state shall be taken and received in all courts, public offices, and official bodies as prima facie evidence of the absence of those documents in the files of the secretary of state.~~

~~(c) The secretary of state's filing of the articles of incorporation is conclusive proof that the incorporators satisfied all conditions precedent to incorporation except in a proceeding by the state to cancel or revoke the incorporation or involuntarily dissolve the corporation~~

A certificate from the secretary of state delivered with a copy of a document filed by the secretary of state is conclusive evidence that the document is on file with the secretary of state.

Sec. 10. 11A V.S.A. § 1.40 is amended to read:
§ 1.40. DEFINITIONS

* * *

(5) "Deliver" ~~includes mail~~ or "delivery" means any method of delivery used in conventional commercial practice, including delivery by hand, mail, commercial delivery, and electronic transmission.

* * *

(25) "Electronic transmission" or "electronically transmitted" means a process of communication not directly involving the physical transfer of paper that is suitable for the retention, retrieval, and reproduction of information by the recipient.

(26) "Meeting" means any structured communications conducted by participants in person or through the use of electronic or telecommunications medium permitting simultaneous or sequentially structured communications for the purpose of reaching a collective agreement.

(27) "Sign" or "signature" includes any manual, facsimile, conformed, or electronic signature.

Sec. 11. 11A V.S.A. § 141(b) and (c) are amended to read:

(b) Notice may be communicated in person; by telephone, voice mail, telegraph, teletype, facsimile, or other form of wire ~~or~~, wireless, or electronic communication; or by mail or private carrier or other method of delivery. If these forms of personal notice are impracticable, notice may be communicated by a newspaper of general circulation in the area where published; or by radio, television, or other form of public broadcast communication.

(c) Notice to shareholders. Written notice by a domestic or foreign corporation to its shareholder, if in a comprehensible form, is effective when:

(1) mailed first class postpaid and correctly addressed to the shareholder's address as shown in the corporation's current record of shareholders; or

(2) electronically transmitted to the shareholder in a manner authorized by the shareholder.

Sec. 12. 11A V.S.A. § 6.01 is amended to read:
§ 6.01. AUTHORIZED SHARES

* * *

(d) ~~The description of the designations, preferences, limitations, and relative rights of share classes in subsection (c) of this section is not exhaustive~~ Terms of shares may be made dependent upon facts objectively ascertainable outside the articles of incorporation in accordance with subsection 1.20(k) of this title.

(e) Any of the terms of shares may vary among holders of the same class or series so long as such variations are expressly set forth in the articles of incorporation.

(f) The description of the designations, preferences, limitations, and relative rights of share classes in subsection (c) of this section is not exhaustive.

Sec.13. 11A V.S.A. § 6.21 is amended to read:
§ 6.21. ISSUANCE OF SHARES

* * *

(b) The board of directors may authorize shares to be issued for consideration consisting of any tangible or intangible property or benefit to the corporation, including cash, promissory notes, services performed, contracts for services performed, or other securities of the corporation. ~~Future services shall not constitute payment or part payment for shares of a corporation.~~

* * *

(e) The corporation may place in escrow shares issued for a contract for future services or benefits or a promissory note, or make other arrangements to restrict the transfer of the shares, and may credit distributions in respect of the shares against their purchase price, until the services are performed, the note is paid, or the benefits are received. If the services are not performed, the note is not paid, or the benefits are not received, the shares escrowed or restricted and the distributions credited may be cancelled in whole or part.

Sec. 14. 11A V.S.A. § 6.24 is amended to read:
§ 6.24. SHARE OPTIONS

~~A corporation may issue rights, options, or warrants for the purchase of shares of the corporation. The board of directors shall determine the terms upon which the rights, options, or warrants are issued, their form and content, and the consideration for which the shares are to be issued. The provisions of sections 8.60 through 8.63 of this title apply in accordance with their terms in the case of transactions involving the issuance of rights, options, or warrants for the purchase of shares to directors. Any transactions involving the issuance of options for the purchase of shares to directors, as such, shall be subject to the approval of the shareholders.~~

(a) A corporation may issue rights, options, or warrants for the purchase of shares or other securities of the corporation. The board of directors shall determine:

(1) the terms upon which the rights, options, or warrants are issued; and

(2) the terms, including the consideration for which the shares or other securities are to be issued.

(b) The authorization by the board of directors for the corporation to issue such rights, options, or warrants constitutes authorization of the issuance of the shares or other securities for which the rights, options, or warrants are exercisable.

(c) The terms and conditions of such rights, options, or warrants, including those outstanding on the effective date of this section, may include, without limitation, restrictions or conditions that:

(1) preclude or limit the exercise, transfer, or receipt of such rights, options, or warrants by any person or persons owning or offering to acquire a specified number or percentage of the outstanding shares or other securities of the corporation or by any transferee or transferees of any such person or persons; or

(2) invalidate or void such rights, options, or warrants held by any such person or persons or any such transferee or transferees.

Sec. 15. 11A V.S.A. § 7.01 is amended to read:
§ 7.01. ANNUAL MEETING

~~(a) A corporation shall hold a meeting of shareholders annually at a time stated in or fixed in accordance with the bylaws.~~

~~(b) Annual shareholders' meetings shall be held in this state, unless permitted in the bylaws of the corporation to be held out of this state. Annual meetings shall be held at the place stated in or fixed in accordance with the bylaws. If no place is stated in or fixed in accordance with the bylaws, annual meetings shall be held at the corporation's principal office. An annual meeting may be conducted by means of any telecommunications mechanism, including video-conference telecommunication.~~

~~(c) The failure to hold an annual meeting at the time stated in or fixed in accordance with a corporation's bylaws does not affect the validity of any corporate action, and shall result not in a forfeiture or dissolution of the corporation.~~

Annual shareholders' meetings shall be held in this state, unless permitted in the bylaws of the corporation to be held outside this state. Annual meetings shall be held at the place stated in or fixed in accordance with the bylaws. If no place is stated in or fixed in accordance with the bylaws, annual meetings shall be held at the corporation's principal office. An annual meeting may be conducted by means of any electronic or telecommunications mechanism, including video-conference telecommunication. The failure to hold an annual meeting at the time stated or fixed in accordance with a corporation's bylaws does not affect the validity of any corporate action.

Sec. 16. 11A V.S.A. § 7.02(c) is amended to read:

(c) Special shareholders' meetings shall be held in this state, unless permitted in the bylaws of the corporation to be held out of this state. Meetings shall be held at the place stated in or fixed in accordance with the bylaws. If no place is stated in or fixed in accordance with the bylaws, annual meetings shall be held at the corporation's principal office. A special meeting may be conducted by means of any electronic or telecommunications mechanism, including video-conference telecommunication.

Sec. 17. 11A V.S.A. § 7.04(a) is amended to read:

(a) Unless the articles of incorporation preclude the taking of action required or permitted by this title without a shareholders' meeting, action required or permitted by this title to be taken at a shareholders' meeting may be taken without a meeting if the action is taken by all the shareholders entitled to vote on the action. Each action must be evidenced by one or more written consents describing the action taken, signed by all the shareholders entitled to vote on the action, and delivered to the corporation for inclusion in the minutes or filed with the corporate records. For purposes of this section, consent evidenced by electronic communications or an electronic record is written consent.

Sec. 18. 11A V.S.A. § 7.32 is added to read:

§ 7.32. SHAREHOLDER AGREEMENTS

(a) An agreement among the shareholders of a corporation that complies with this section is effective among the shareholders and the corporation even though it is inconsistent with one or more other provisions of this title in that it:

(1) eliminates the board of directors or restricts the discretion or powers of the board of directors;

(2) governs the authorization or making of distributions whether or not in proportion to ownership of shares, subject to the limitations in section 6.40 of this title;

(3) establishes who shall be directors or officers of the corporation, or their terms of office or manner of selection or removal;

(4) governs, in general or in regard to specific matters, the exercise or division of voting power by or between the shareholders and directors or by or among any of them, including the use of weighted voting rights or director proxies;

(5) establishes the terms and conditions of any agreement for the transfer or use of property or the provision of services between the corporation and any shareholder, director, officer, or employee of the corporation or among any of them;

(6) transfers to one or more shareholders or other persons all or part of the authority to exercise the corporate powers or to manage the business and affairs of the corporation, including the resolution of any issue about which there exists a deadlock among directors or shareholders;

(7) requires dissolution of the corporation at the request of one or more of the shareholders or upon the occurrence of a specified event; or

(8) otherwise governs the exercise of the corporate powers or the management of the business and affairs of the corporation or the relationship among the shareholders, the directors, and the corporation, or among any of them, and is not contrary to public policy.

(b) An agreement authorized by this section shall be:

(1) set forth:

(A) in the articles of incorporation or bylaws and approved by all persons who are shareholders at the time of the agreement; or

(B) in a written agreement that is signed by all persons who are shareholders at the time of the agreement and is made known to the corporation;

(2) subject to amendment only by the holders of a majority of each class of the corporation's issued and outstanding capital stock, with each class voting as a separate group, unless the agreement provides otherwise; and

(3) valid for 10 years, unless the agreement provides otherwise.

(c) The existence of an agreement authorized by this section shall be noted conspicuously on the front or back of each certificate for outstanding shares or on the information statement required by subsection 6.26(b) of this title. If at the time of the agreement the corporation has shares outstanding represented by certificates, the corporation shall recall the outstanding certificates and issue substitute certificates that comply with this subsection. The failure to note the existence of the agreement on the certificate or information statement shall not affect the validity of the agreement or any action taken pursuant to it. Any purchaser of shares who, at the time of purchase, did not have knowledge of the existence of the agreement shall be entitled to rescission of the purchase. A purchaser shall be deemed to have knowledge of the existence of the agreement if its existence is noted on the certificate or information statement for the shares in compliance with this subsection and, if the shares are not represented by a certificate, the information statement is delivered to the purchaser at or prior to the time of the purchase of the shares. An action to enforce the right of rescission authorized by this subsection must be commenced within the earlier of 90 days after discovery of the existence of the agreement or two years after the time of the purchase of the shares.

(d) An agreement authorized by this section shall cease to be effective when the corporation becomes a public corporation. If the agreement ceases to be effective for any reason, the board of directors may, if the agreement is contained or referred to in the corporation's articles of incorporation or bylaws, adopt an amendment to the articles of incorporation or bylaws, without shareholder action, to delete the agreement and any references to it.

(e) An agreement authorized by this section that limits the discretion or powers of the board of directors shall relieve the directors of, and impose upon the person or persons in whom such discretion or powers are vested, liability for acts or omissions imposed by law on directors to the extent that the discretion or powers of the directors are limited by the agreement.

(f) The existence or performance of an agreement authorized by this section shall not be a ground for imposing personal liability on any shareholder for the acts or debts of the corporation, even if the agreement or its performance treats the corporation as if it were a partnership or results in failure to observe the corporate formalities otherwise applicable to the matters governed by the agreement.

(g) Incorporators or subscribers for shares may act as shareholders with respect to an agreement authorized by this section if no shares have been issued when the agreement is made.

Sec. 19. 11A V.S.A. § 8.03(a) amended to read:

(a) A board of directors of a corporation which is not a close corporation dispensing with a board of directors pursuant to section 20.08 of this title must consist of ~~three~~ one or more individuals, with the number specified in or fixed in accordance with the articles of incorporation or bylaws. ~~If the number of shareholders in any corporation is less than three, the~~ The number of directors may be ~~as few as the number of shareholders~~ increased or decreased from time to time by amendment to, or in the manner provided in, the articles of incorporation or the bylaws.

Sec. 20. 11A V.S.A. § 8.20 is amended to read:

§ 8.20. MEETINGS

(a) The board of directors may hold regular or special meetings, as defined in subdivision 1.40(26) of this title, in or ~~out of~~ outside this state.

(b) The board of directors may permit any or all directors to participate in a regular or special meeting by, or conduct the meeting through the use of, any means of communication, including an electronic, telecommunications, and video- or audio-conferencing conference telephone call, by which all directors participating may simultaneously ~~hear~~ communicate with each other during the meeting. A director participating in a meeting by this means is deemed to be present in person at the meeting.

Sec. 21. 11A V.S.A. § 8.40 is amended to read:
§ 8.40. ~~REQUIRED~~ OFFICERS

(a) A corporation has the officers described in its bylaws or appointed by the board of directors in accordance with the bylaws~~, provided that a corporation shall have a president and a secretary. Any two or more offices may be held by the same person, except the offices of president and secretary, unless the corporation is a professional corporation organized under chapter 3 or 4 of Title 11~~.

(b) ~~A duly appointed~~ The board of directors may elect individuals to fill one or more offices of the corporations. An officer may appoint one or more officers or assistant officers if authorized by the bylaws or the board of directors.

(c) The bylaws or the board of directors shall ~~delegate~~ assign to one of the officers responsibility for preparing the minutes of the directors' and shareholders' meetings and for authenticating and maintaining the records of the corporation required to be kept under subsections 16.01(a) and 16.10(e) of this title.

* * *

~~(e) An individual who holds more than one office may execute, acknowledge or verify in more than one capacity any document required to be executed, acknowledged or verified by the holders of two or more officers.~~

Sec. 22. 11A V.S.A. § 8.60 is amended to read:
§ 8.60. DEFINITIONS

For purposes of this subchapter:

~~(1) "Conflicting interest" with respect to a corporation means the interest a director of the corporation has respecting a transaction effected or proposed to be effected by the corporation (or by a subsidiary of the corporation or any other entity in which the corporation has a controlling interest) if~~

~~(A) whether or not the transaction is brought before the board of directors of the corporation for action, the director knows at the time of commitment that he or she or a related person is a party to the transaction or has a beneficial financial interest in or so closely linked to the transaction and of such financial significance to the director or a related person that the interest would reasonably be expected to exert an influence on the director's judgment if he or she were called upon to vote on the transaction; or~~

~~(B) the transaction is brought (or is of such character and significance to the corporation that it would in the normal course be brought) before the board of directors of the corporation for action, and the director knows at the time of commitment that any of the following persons is either a party to the transaction or has a beneficial financial interest in or so closely linked to the transaction and of such financial significance to the person that the interest would reasonably be expected to exert an influence on the director's judgment if he or she were called upon to vote on the transaction:~~

~~(i) an entity (other than the corporation) of which the director is a director, general partner, agent, or employee;~~

~~(ii) a person that controls one or more of the entities specified in subdivision (i) of this subdivision or an entity that is controlled by, or is under common control with, one or more of the entities specified in subdivision (i); or~~

~~(iii) an individual who is a general partner, principal, or employer of the director.~~

~~(2) "Director's conflicting interest transaction" with respect to a corporation means a transaction effected or proposed to be effected by the corporation (or by a subsidiary of the corporation or any other entity in which the corporation has a controlling interest) respecting which a director of the corporation has a conflicting interest.~~

~~(3) "Related person" of a director means (A) the spouse (or a parent or sibling thereof) of the director, or a child, grandchild, sibling, parent (or spouse of any thereof) of the director, or an individual having the same home as the director, or a trust or estate of which an individual specified in this subdivision (A) is a substantial beneficiary; or (B) a trust, estate, incompetent, conservatee, or minor of which the director is a fiduciary.~~

~~(4) "Required disclosure" means disclosure by the director who has a conflicting interest of (A) the existence and nature of his or her conflicting interest, and (B) all facts known to him or her respecting the subject matter of the transaction that an ordinarily prudent person would reasonably believe to be material to a judgment about whether or not to proceed with the transaction.~~

~~(5) "Time of commitment" respecting a transaction means the time when the transaction is consummated or, if made pursuant to contract, the time when the corporation (or its subsidiary or~~

~~the entity in which it has a controlling interest) becomes contractually obligated so that its unilateral withdrawal from the transaction would entail significant loss, liability, or other damage.~~

(1) "Control" including the term "controlled by" means:

(A) having the power, directly or indirectly, to elect or remove a majority of the members of the board of directors or other governing body of an entity whether through the ownership of voting shares or interests, by contract, or otherwise; or

(B) being subject to a majority of the risk of loss from the entity's activities or entitled to receive a majority of the entity's residual returns.

(2) "Director's conflicting interest transaction" means a transaction effected or proposed to be effected by the corporation or by an entity controlled by the corporation that at the relevant time the director:

(A) was a party to; or

(B) had knowledge of and a material financial interest known to the director; or

(C) knew that a related person was a party or had a material financial interest.

(3) "Fair to the corporation" means, for purposes of subdivision 8.61(b)(3) of this title, that the transaction as a whole was beneficial to the corporation, taking into appropriate account whether it was:

(A) fair in terms of the director's dealings with the corporation; and

(B) comparable to what might have been obtainable in an arm's length transaction, given the consideration paid or received by the corporation.

(4) "Material financial interest" means a financial interest in a transaction that would reasonably be expected to impair the objectivity of the director's judgment when participating in action on the authorization of the transaction.

(5) "Related person" means:

(A) the director's spouse;

(B) a child, stepchild, grandchild, parent, stepparent, grandparent, sibling, step sibling, half sibling, aunt, uncle, niece, or nephew (or spouse of any thereof) of the director or of the director's spouse;

(C) an individual living in the same home as the director;

(D) an entity, other than the corporation or an entity controlled by the corporation, controlled by the director or any person specified in this subdivision;

(E) a domestic or foreign:

(i) business or nonprofit corporation (other than the corporation or an entity controlled by the corporation) of which the director is a director;

(ii) unincorporated entity of which the director is a general partner or a member of the governing body; or

(iii) individual, trust, or estate for whom or of which the director is a trustee, guardian, personal representative, or like fiduciary; or

(F) a person that is, or an entity that is controlled by, an employer of the director.

(6) "Relevant time" means:

(A) the time at which the directors' action respecting the transaction is taken in compliance with section 8.62 of this title; or

(B) if the transaction is not brought before the board of directors of the corporation or its committee for action under section 8.62 of this title, at the time the corporation, or an entity controlled by the corporation, becomes legally obligated to consummate the transaction.

(7) "Required disclosure" means disclosure of:

(A) the existence and nature of the director's conflicting interest; and

(B) all facts known to the director respecting the subject matter of the transaction that a director free of such conflicting interest would reasonably believe to be material in deciding whether to proceed with the transaction.

Sec. 23. 11A V.S.A. § 8.61 is amended to read:

§ 8.61. JUDICIAL ACTION

~~(a) A transaction effected or proposed to be effected by a corporation (or by a subsidiary of the corporation or any other entity in which the corporation has a controlling interest) that is not a director's conflicting interest transaction may not be enjoined, set aside, or give rise to an award of damages or other sanctions, in a proceeding by a shareholder or by or in the right of the corporation, because a director of the corporation, or any person with whom or~~

~~which he or she has a personal, economic, or other association, has an interest in the transaction.~~

~~(b) A director's conflicting interest transaction may not be enjoined, set aside, or give rise to an award of damages or other sanctions, in a proceeding by a shareholder or by or in the right of the corporation, because the director, or any person with whom or which he or she has a personal, economic, or other association, has an interest in the transaction, if:~~

~~(1) directors' action respecting the transaction was at any time taken in compliance with section 8.62 of this subchapter;~~

~~(2) shareholders' action respecting the transaction was at any time taken in compliance with section 8.63 of this subchapter; or~~

~~(3) the transaction, judged according to the circumstances at the time of commitment, is established to have been fair to the corporation.~~

(a) A transaction effected or proposed to be effected by the corporation, or by an entity controlled by the corporation, may not be the subject of equitable relief, or give rise to an award of damages or other sanctions against a director of the corporation, in a proceeding by a shareholder or by or in the right of the corporation, on the ground that the director has an interest respecting the transaction, if it is not a director's conflicting interest transaction.

(b) A director's conflicting interest transaction may not be the subject of equitable relief, or give rise to an award of damages or other sanctions against a director of the corporation, in a proceeding by a shareholder, or by or in the right of the corporation, on the ground that the director has an interest respecting the transaction, if:

(1) the directors' action respecting the transaction was taken in compliance with section 8.62 of this title at any time; or

(2) the shareholders' action respecting the transaction was taken in compliance with section 8.63 of this title at any time; or

(3) the transaction, judged according to the circumstances at the relevant time, is established to have been fair to the corporation.

Sec. 24. 11A V.S.A. § 8.62 is amended to read:

§ 8.62. DIRECTORS' ACTION

~~(a) Directors' action respecting a transaction is effective for purposes of section 8.61(b)(1) of this subchapter if the transaction received the affirmative vote of a majority (but no fewer than two)~~

~~of those qualified directors on the board of directors or on a duly empowered committee of the board who voted on the transaction after either required disclosure to them (to the extent the information was not known by them) or compliance with subsection (b) of this section; provided that action by a committee is so effective only if:~~

~~(1) all its members are qualified directors; and~~

~~(2) its members are either all the qualified directors on the board or are appointed by the affirmative vote of a majority of the qualified directors on the board.~~

~~(b) If a director has a conflicting interest respecting a transaction, but neither he nor she nor a related person of the director specified in section 8.60(3) of this subchapter is a party to the transaction, and if the director has a duty under law or professional canon, or a duty of confidentiality to another person, respecting information relating to the transaction such that the director may not make the disclosure described in section 8.60(4), then disclosure is sufficient for purposes of subsection (a) of this section if the director (1) discloses to the directors voting on the transaction the existence and nature of his or her conflicting interest and informs them of the character and limitations imposed by that duty before their vote on the transaction, and (2) plays no part, directly or indirectly, in their deliberations or vote.~~

~~(c) A majority (but no fewer than two) of all the qualified directors on the board of directors, or on the committee, constitutes a quorum for purposes of action that complies with this section. Directors' action that otherwise complies with this section is not affected by the presence or vote of a director who is not a qualified director.~~

~~(d) For purposes of this section, "qualified director" means, with respect to a director's conflicting interest transaction, any director who does not have either (1) a conflicting interest respecting the transaction, or (2) a familial, financial, professional, or employment relationship with a second director who does have a conflicting interest respecting the transaction, which relationship would, in the circumstances, reasonably be expected to exert an influence on the first director's judgment when voting on the transaction.~~

(a) Directors' action respecting a director's conflicting interest transaction is effective for purposes of subdivision 8.61(b)(1) of this title if the transaction has been authorized by the affirmative vote of a majority, but no fewer than two, of the qualified directors who voted on the transaction after required disclosure by the conflicted director of information not already known by such qualified directors, or after modified disclosure in compliance with subsection (b) of this section, provided that:

(1) the qualified directors have deliberated and voted outside the presence of and without the participation by any other director; and

(2) where the action has been taken by a committee, all members of the committee were qualified directors, and either:

(A) the committee was composed of all the qualified directors on the board of directors; or

(B) the members of the committee were appointed by the affirmative vote of a majority of the qualified directors on the board.

(b) Notwithstanding subsection (a) of this section, when a transaction is a director's conflicting interest transaction only because a related person described in subdivisions 8.60(5)(E) and (F) of this title is a party to or has a material financial interest in the transaction, the conflicted director is not obligated to make required disclosure to the extent that the director reasonably believes that doing so would violate a duty imposed under law, a legally enforceable obligation of confidentiality, or a professional ethics rule, provided that the conflicted director discloses to the qualified directors voting on the transaction:

(1) all information required to be disclosed that is not so violative;

(2) the existence and nature of the director's conflicting interest; and

(3) the nature of the conflicted director's duty not to disclose the confidential information.

(c) A majority, but no fewer than two, of all the qualified directors on the board of directors or on the committee constitutes a quorum for purposes of action that complies with this section.

(d) Where directors' action under this section does not satisfy a quorum or voting requirement applicable to the authorization of the transaction by reason of the articles of incorporation, the bylaws, or a provision of law, independent action to satisfy those authorization requirements must be taken by the board of directors or a committee, in which action directors who are not qualified directors may participate.

Sec. 25. 11A V.S.A. § 8.63 is amended to read:
§ 8.63. SHAREHOLDERS' ACTION

~~(a) Shareholders' action respecting a transaction is effective for purposes of section 8.61(b)(2) of this subchapter if a majority of the votes entitled to be cast by the holders of all qualified shares was cast in favor of the transaction after (1) notice to shareholders describing the director's conflicting interest transaction, (2) provision of the information referred to in subsection (d) of this section, and (3) required disclosure to the shareholders who voted on the transaction (to the extent the information was not known by them).~~

~~(b) For purposes of this section, "qualified shares" mean any shares entitled to vote with respect to the director's conflicting interest transaction except shares that, to the knowledge, before the vote, of the secretary (or other officer or agent of the corporation authorized to tabulate votes), are beneficially owned (or the voting of which is controlled) by a director who has a conflicting interest respecting the transaction or by a related person of the director, or both.~~

~~(c) A majority of the votes entitled to be cast by the holders of all qualified shares constitutes a quorum for purposes of action that complies with this section. Subject to the provisions of subsections (d) and (e) of this section, shareholders' action that otherwise complies with this section is not affected by the presence of holders, or the voting, of shares that are not qualified shares.~~

~~(d) For purposes of compliance with subsection (a) of this section, a director who has a conflicting interest respecting the transaction shall, before the shareholders' vote, inform the secretary (or other officer or agent of the corporation authorized to tabulate votes) of the number, and the identity of persons holding or controlling the vote, of all shares that the director knows are beneficially owned (or the voting of which is controlled) by the director or by a related person of the director, or both.~~

~~(e) If a shareholders' vote does not comply with subsection (a) of this section solely because of a failure of a director to comply with subsection (d), and if the director establishes that his or her failure did not determine and was not intended by him or her to~~

~~influence the outcome of the vote, the court may, with or without further proceedings respecting section 8.61(b)(3) of this subchapter, take such action respecting the transaction and the director, and give such effect, if any, to the shareholders' vote, as it considers appropriate in the circumstances.~~

(a) Shareholders' action respecting a director's conflicting interest transaction is effective for purposes of subdivision 8.61(b)(2) of this title if a majority of the votes cast by the holders of all qualified shares is in favor of the transaction after:

(1) notice to shareholders describing the action to be taken respecting the transaction;

(2) provision to the corporation of the information referred to in subsection (b) of this section; and

(3) communication of the information that is the subject of required disclosure to the shareholders entitled to vote on the transaction, to the extent the information is not known by them.

(b) A director who has a conflicting interest respecting the transaction shall, before the shareholders' vote, inform the secretary or other officer or agent of the corporation authorized to tabulate votes, in writing, of the number of shares that the director knows are not qualified shares under subsection (c) of this section and the identity of the holders of those shares.

(c) For purposes of this section:

(1) "Holder" means and "held by" refers to shares held by both a record shareholder, as defined in subdivision 13.01(7) of this title, and a beneficial shareholder, as defined in subdivision 13.01(2) of this title;

(2) "Qualified shares" means all shares entitled to be voted with respect to the transaction except for shares that the secretary or other officer or agent of the corporation authorized to tabulate votes either knows, or under subsection (b) of this section is notified, are held by:

(A) a director who has a conflicting interest respecting the transaction; or

(B) a related person of the director, excluding a person described in subdivision 8.60(5)(F) of this title.

(d) A majority of the votes entitled to be cast by the holders of all qualified shares constitutes a quorum for purposes of compliance with this section. Subject to the provisions of subsection (e) of this section, shareholders' action that otherwise complies with this section is not affected by the presence of holders, or by the voting, of shares that are not qualified shares.

(e) If a shareholders' vote does not comply with subsection (a) of this section solely because of a director's failure to comply with subsection (b) of this section, and if the director establishes that the failure was not intended to influence and did not in fact determine the outcome of the vote, the court may take such action respecting the transaction and the director, and may give such effect, if any, to the shareholders' vote, as the court considers appropriate in the circumstances.

(f) Where shareholders' action under this section does not satisfy a quorum or voting requirement applicable to the authorization of the transaction by reason of the articles of incorporation, the bylaws, or a provision of law, independent action to satisfy those authorization requirements must be taken by the shareholders, in which action shares that are not qualified shares may participate.

Sec. 26. 11A V.S.A. § 12.02(a) is amended to read:

(a) ~~A corporation may sell, lease, exchange, or otherwise dispose of all, or substantially all, of its property (with or without the good will), otherwise than in the usual and regular course of business, on the terms and conditions and for the consideration determined by the corporation's board of directors, if the board of directors proposes and its shareholders approve the proposed transaction~~ A sale, lease, exchange, or other disposition of assets, other than a disposition described in section 12.01 of this title, requires approval of the corporation's shareholders if the disposition would leave the corporation without a significant continuing business activity. If a corporation retains a business activity that represented at least 25 percent of the total assets at the end of the most recently completed fiscal year and 25 percent of either income from continuing operations before taxes or revenues from continuing operations for that fiscal year, in each case of the corporation and its subsidiaries on a consolidated basis, the corporation will conclusively be deemed to have retained a significant continuing business activity.

Sec. 27. 11A V.S.A. § 16.01(d) and (e) are amended to read:

(d) A corporation shall maintain its records in written form or in another form, including electronic form, capable of conversion into written form within a reasonable time.

(e) A corporation shall keep a copy of the following records at its principal office (or, if none in this state, then the registered office):

* * *

(5) all written <u>or electronic</u> communications to shareholders generally within the past three years, including the financial statements furnished for the past three years under section 16.20 of this title;

* * *

APPENDIX B

Example Client Intake Sheet

Interview Sheet: Information for Formation of a Digital LLC/Virtual Corporation

Client: ____

Client's phone number: ______________________________

Client's e-mail address: _____________________________

Client no: ____

Date of checklist:

I. SUITABILITY

Client advised on the perceived suitability of Digital LLC/Virtual Incorporation and alternatives discussed?

II. CURRENT STATUS

____ New Digital LLC

____ Merger or other conversion of existing entity

If existing entity:

A. Name of existing entity: ____________________

B. Type of entity: ____________________

C. State of formation: ____________________

D. Type of formation documents: ____________________

E. Desire to pattern operating agreement after existing documents: ____________________

III. DIGITAL LLC FORMATION DETAILS

A. Information needed for Articles of Organization

1. Proposed Company name: ____________________
2. Alternate names: ____________________
3. Has name been reserved? Yes ___ No ___
4. Date verified or reserved: ____________________
5. Date reservation expires: ____________________
6. Name must be available for use in the following states:

   ____
7. Is consent to use name necessary? Yes ___ No ___
8. Plan to conduct business under a different name? Yes ___ No ___

If yes, a Fictitious Business Name Statement will need to be filed and published. Please state the fictitious name and each county where you contemplate doing business.

Fictitious name: ____________________

County(ies): ____________________

If you already have a Fictitious Business Name Statement on file, do you wish it to be assigned to the corporation? Yes ___ No ___

Filed by: ____________________ Date of filing: ____________________

County where filed: ____________________

9. Latest date on which the Company is to dissolve: ____

____

10. Name and address of the initial agent for the service of process: ________________________________

____

11. Management roles at time of formation: ____________

____

____

12. Concept of how management might change and evolve over time: ________________________

____

____

B. Optional provisions
   1. Limitations on the Company's business activity:

   ____

   ____

   2. Limitations on Company's powers:

   ____

   ____

   3. Provisions governing the admission of members:

   ____

   ____

   4. Any events that would cause the dissolution of the Company:

   ____

   ____

   5. Limitations on the authority of managers or members to bind the Company:

   ____

   ____

6. Expectations regarding ownership of intellectual property of the contributors created in the course of Company projects?

___

___

7. Payments of net revenues of the Company to members to be based upon capital/property/expertise/reputation/rating system/other?

___

___

8. Voting of members based upon capital/property/expertise/reputation/rating system/other?

___

___

9. Transferability of members' Company interests:

___

___

10. How remaining assets will be distributed upon dissolution?

___

___

11. How a member's active status may be terminated?

___

___

12. Authorization to sign contracts on behalf of the Company:

___

___

13. Other provisions:

___

___

C. Additional information

1. Principal place of business:

Address: ______________________________

City: ______________ County: ______________

State: ______________ Zip: ______________

Telephone number: ______________________

2. Additional location:

Address: ______________________________

City: ______________ County: ______________

State: ______________ Zip: ______________

Telephone number: ______________________

IV. OWNERSHIP

A. Initial founders

Member A

Full legal name: ______________________________

Place of organization if a legal entity or place of residency and nationality if an individual: ______________________

Address: ______________________________

Telephone number (home): ______________________

Telephone number (office): ______________________

Federal taxpayer I.D. number: ______________________

Percent share of ownership in Company: ______________

Type and amount of initial contribution: ______________

Description of property used for initial contribution: __________

____

Description of services contributed for initial contribution: ______

____

Member B

Full legal name: ______________________________________

Place of organization if a legal entity or place of residency and nationality if an individual: ______________________________

Address: ______________________________________

Telephone number (home): ______________________________

Telephone number (office): ______________________________

Federal taxpayer I.D. number: ___________________________

Percent share of ownership in Company: ___________________

Type and amount of initial contribution: ___________________

Description of property used for initial contribution: _________

____

Description of services contributed for initial contribution: _____

____

Member C

Full legal name: ______________________________________

Place of organization if a legal entity or place of residency and nationality if an individual: ______________________________

Address: ______________________________________

Telephone number (home): ______________________________

Telephone number (office): ______________________________

Federal taxpayer I.D. number: ___________________________

Percent share of ownership in Company: ___________________

Type and amount of initial contribution: ___________________

Description of property used for initial contribution: _________

____

Description of services contributed for initial contribution: _____

____

V. BUSINESS INFORMATION

A. Type of business of the company: ____________________

B. List any special permits, licenses, or approvals required by the corporation to conduct its business: ____________

C. Proposed date for formation of company: ____________

D. Accounting information

1. Fiscal year of company:

   Ending: __________ (day) ________ (month)

2. Method of accounting for corporation: (check one)

   Cash _______ Accrual _______ Other ________

E. Accountant

Name: ____

Address: ______________________________________

City: ________________ County: ________________

State: ________________ Zip: __________________

Telephone number: ______________________________

E-mail: _______________________________________

F. Bank

Name: ____

Address: (branch) ______________________________

City: ________________ County: ________________

State: ________________ Zip: __________________

Telephone number: ______________________________

G. IRS employee I.D. number information

1. Approximate peak number of employees anticipated in the next twelve months: ______________________

2. First date wages will be paid to employees: _________

3. To whom do you sell most of your products or services? ____________________________________

Business establishments: ______ General public: ______

Other (specify): ______________________________

4. Have you ever applied for an identification number for this or any other business?

   Yes ____ No ____

   If yes, list the name of the business. Also list the approximate date, the city and state where the application was filed, and the previous number if known: ______________________________

   ____

   ____

5. Owner's Social Security number: ______________

H. Date of annual meeting: ______________________

I. Pre-incorporation advances

1. Has anyone, or will anyone, advance funds to or for the benefit of the company for any purpose other than the payment of initial organization expenses?

   Yes ____ No ____

2. If yes, please identify such persons and the dates, amounts, and purposes of such advances:

   ____

   ____

How will the company reimburse these advances?

Cash: ________ Shares: ________ Notes: ________

APPENDIX C

Example Checklist for Incorporation

Client: ____

- Initial Meeting
  - ____ Incorporation Package Fees
  - ____ Attorney-Client Fee Agreement
  - ____ Interview Sheet for Digital LLC/Virtual Incorporation
- Name Search
  - ____ Secretary of State business search
  - ____ USPTO search
  - ____ Internet search
  - ____ Domain name availability search
- Articles of Organization
  - ____ Form of Articles of Organization
  - ____ Information Needed for Filing of Articles of Organization

- Operating Agreement
  - ____ Form of Operating Agreement
  - ____ Guide for Advising on Operating Agreement
- Company Records Book (can be kept electronically)
  - ____ Articles
  - ____ Operating Agreement
  - ____ Minutes of actions taken by its members
  - ____ Share information
- Share Ownership Recording (Cap Table)
  - ____ Share ledger—ownership records with copies of all share issues
- Federal Tax ID Number (FEIN)
  - ____ Obtain ASAP after LLC is formed
  - ____ IRS Form SS-4—http://www.irs.gov/pub/irs-pdf/fss4.pdf
  - ____ Questions—call IRS at (800) 829-4933
- State Employer Identification Number

APPENDIX D

Example Operating Agreement

Vermont Virtual Company, an organization (located at http://www.vermontvirtual.org) posted the following draft template Operating Agreement at http://vermontvirtual.org/Picking_the_Operating_Agreement on September 2, 2008.

Limited Liability Company Operating Agreement

Member-Managed Limited Liability Company

Each Member of the Company agrees to be bound by the following provisions:

Work Product. All Members irrevocably transfer and assign all right, title and interest to any work product created (now or in the future) in the course of Company projects to the Company. In creating any work product for the Company or otherwise performing services for the Company, Members shall be independent contractors of the Company.

Point Allocation. At the end of the first full calendar quarter following the creation of the Company (the "Initial Contribution Period" or "ICP"), the founding member(s) (the "Founder(s)") shall determine the number of Points to be allocated to each Member of the Company (including the Founder(s)) with respect to contributions made during that Period. At the end of each calendar quarter ("Period") after the ICP, each Member will be entitled Point Allocation Votes ("PAVs"), to be used to allocate points ("Points") to other Members, in a number equal to the Points the Member was allocated in the immediately preceding Period. Members who have received Points in the immediately preceding Period shall be deemed "Active Members." Only Active Members shall be eligible to vote on Company decisions, though Active Member status is not required to receive Points. From time to time, the Active Members may decide to multiply all valid Points by a factor designed to adjust the number of Points in light of the size of the membership entitled to receive Points or for other reasons.

Points Received. Points received by each Member will be cumulative throughout the life of the Company; but if no Points are received by a Member for three consecutive Periods, all Points previously accumulated by such Member shall become void.

Payment of Revenues. The Active Members shall decide the amount of revenues to be paid out to Members ("Member Payments") during any Period. Revenues shall be paid to Members in proportion to the number of valid Points held by each Member as a percentage of all valid Points outstanding. No Member Payments may be made to the extent that they would cause the Company to be unable to pay its debts as they become due in the ordinary course of business. All Member Payments shall be deemed compensation to the Members for their contributions to the Company as independent contractors.

Liability of Members. The debts, obligations and liabilities of the Company are solely the debts, obligations and liabilities of the Company. A Member will not be personally liable for a debt, obligation or liability of the Company solely by reason of being or acting as a Member or Active Member.

Decisions by Members. Except for amendment of this Agreement, all decisions and any consent, approval, or action of the Company may be taken by means of a majority of the votes cast by Active Members entitled to vote and voting during a period of at least one week. Notice of any pending decision shall be provided on the Company web site. Each Active Member may cast a number of votes equal to the number of Points awarded to such Active Member in the immediately preceding Period. The Active Members (or the Founders during the ICP) may choose to designate one or more agents to act on behalf of the Company.

Service Providers. The Company shall engage VVCC as its service provider to provide services on such terms as are agreed upon by the Founder(s) and VVCC. During the ICP, the Founder(s) may also cause the Company to engage accountants, lawyers and other service providers on behalf of the Company.

Founder(s) Agreement. During the ICP, the Founder(s) may cause the Company to enter into an agreement with the Founders on such terms as are agreed upon by the Founder(s) and are disclosed at the Company web site.

Tax Election. The Company shall elect to be treated for federal and state income tax purposes as a "Subchapter C corporation." The Founder(s) or their designee(s) shall be the shareholder(s) (the "Shareholder(s)") of the Company for federal and state income tax purposes absent a decision of the Members to designate another person as the Shareholder(s).

Capital. The Founder(s) shall contribute as capital such amounts as the Founder(s) deem appropriate. During the ICP, the Founder(s) may cause the Company to accept additional loans on terms approved by the Founder(s). After the ICP, the Company may accept such other loans as are approved by the Active Members.

Amendments. Any Active Member may propose an amendment of this Agreement. Approval of such amendment shall require an affirmative two-thirds vote of the Active Members of the Company who vote during the specified period (not less than two weeks following notice of the proposal).

Choice of Law. The law of the State of Vermont shall govern this Agreement.

Arbitration. The Members agree that any and all disputes related to or arising from this Agreement will be resolved through online arbitration under the rules of and as facilitated by Virtual Mediation and Arbitration System, LLC.

Non-transferability. Any interest of a Member in the Company created under this Agreement will be non-transferable and shall terminate upon the death of the Member.

Dissolution. Upon dissolution and liquidation of the Company and after payment of all debts and liabilities, any remaining assets will be distributed in proportion to the valid points held by the Active Members.

Registered Agent. Gravel and Shea is the Company's registered agent in the State of Vermont. The registered agent's office is located at 76 St. Paul Street, Burlington, VT 05401.

Designated Office. The location of the principal place of business of the Company will be the office of the Company's registered agent.

Termination of Access and Active Membership. The right of a Member to access the Company site, and a Member's status as an Active Member, may be terminated by vote of a majority of the votes cast by voting Active Members within 2 weeks after such termination is proposed by any Active Member.

Contracts With Third Parties. With the exception of agreements signed by the Founder(s) with the service providers identified above, and the agreement between the Company and the Founder(s) described above, no Member may sign a contract on behalf of the Company unless expressly authorized by a decision of the Members to do so, and any contract signed without such express authorization will be invalid.

Integration. This agreement constitutes the entire operating agreement among the parties.

> **ACKNOWLEDGMENT OF ARBITRATION. This agreement contains an agreement to arbitrate. After entering into this agreement, I understand that I will not be able to bring a lawsuit concerning any dispute that may arise which is covered by the arbitration agreement, unless it involves a question of constitutional or civil rights. Instead, I agree to submit any such dispute to an impartial arbitrator as described above.**

INDEX

ABOUT THE AUTHORS

Paul S. Gillies

Paul S. Gillies is a partner in the Montpelier, Vermont, law firm of Tarrant, Marks & Gillies. He served as Vermont Deputy Secretary of State (1981–1993) and is presently moderator of the Berlin, Vermont, town meeting. He writes a regular column on Vermont judicial and legal history in the *Vermont Bar Journal*. He served on various committees responsible for drafting Vermont's business laws. He has a varied law practice that concentrates on the nexus between history and law. He coedited the *Records of the Vermont Council of Censors* (1991) with D. Gregory Sanford, and with James H. Douglas coauthored *A Book of Opinions* (1993), on laws and practices affecting Vermont municipalities.

Linsey Krolik

Linsey Krolik is a technology, media, and business lawyer in Silicon Valley, California. She has operated her solo law practice since 2004, providing outsourced general counsel, technology and content licensing, and business formation services to a range of clients from small businesses and start-up companies to established, large corporations. Her clients include a variety of businesses, including microprocessors, computer hardware, software, Internet, wireless, blog, and medical device companies. Before starting her solo practice, Linsey was Corporate Counsel for ARM, Inc., a United Kingdom–based intellectual property company. Prior to that, she worked in both legal and business roles for a variety of tech companies in the Silicon Valley, including Palm, Inc., OmniSky Corporation, and 3Com Corporation.

Linsey writes a blog called Whereas (http://www.kroliklegal.com/whereas), about legal issues in technology, as well as maintaining and contributing to several other blogs. She spoke at

BlogHer'08 on the topic of legal issues with blogging in the "Taking Care of Business" session. Linsey holds a combination JD/MBA degree from Santa Clara University School of Law with a concentration in High Technology Law. She has been a member of the California State Bar Association since 2002. Linsey is active in her community, serving as a board member for several local organizations.

Julie Tower-Pierce

Julie Tower-Pierce is a lawyer admitted to practice in Vermont and the District of Columbia. She is a former associate at Tarrant, Marks & Gillies in Montpelier, Vermont, and past adjunct professor at Norwich University, where she taught courses in Cybercrime and Cyberlaw. Julie's legal background includes work in the areas of business and privacy law, regulatory compliance, and civil and criminal litigation. She is author of the American Bar Association Best Seller, *Staying at Home, Staying in the Law: A Guide to Remaining Active in the Legal Profession While Pursuing Your Dreams.*

Julie served as Articles editor of the *Vermont Law Review,* on the editorial boards of the American Bar Association's Young Lawyer and the Norwich University Journal of Information Assurance, and as a contributing editor to the SANS Business Law and Computer Security course. Her writing and legal/technology commentary have appeared in a number of publications, including SANS NewsBites, *Information Security Magazine,* Vermont's *Strictly Business,* and *The Miami Herald.* She blogs at Darling Hill (http://www.darlinghill.com). Julie holds a bachelor's degree from Dalhousie University, and a master's degree and JD from Vermont Law School.